TRANSITION

Pastor Robert,

Accelerated blessings!!

Eric

3/6/16

MASTERING LIFE'S
MOVEMENTS

STAN ELLIS

DIVINE HOUSE
B O O K S

ACKNOWLEDGMENTS

Her grace, virtue and trustworthiness reflect her very essence. My advancements are a reflection of my desire to become a man that she's worthy of. Without ever trying to change me she inspired me to change. To my wife Evelyn—thanks for being who you are.

INTRODUCTION

There are times when your life is only as powerful as the words that you have at your disposal. When you are trying to go to a new place in life you need new words to help you get there. You need words that are empowering and words that are liberating. Words that help you define where you are going. There is something powerful about being able to articulate your present experience and your present journey. Being able to do so with precision and clarity gives you a floor on which to stand. It gives you a level of confidence to aid you in your navigation to your next season.

It could very well be that one of the words you are looking for is "transition." It is very conceivable that the meaning behind your current season is that "you are in transition." God highlights particular words for particular seasons. There are certain words that have emerged in our generation that have infused tremendous power into the lives of countless people. Words like "destiny" and "purpose." God gives significant power to certain words during distinct times. The better your understanding and articulation of a word— the greater power that word will have in your life. I believe "transition" is one of the words that God is highlighting for this generation. The revelation of the process called transition will revolutionize your perspective, and bring calm and clarity to many of the movements that life will take you through.

The greatest season of change in my life felt like a mystery to me until I heard the word "transition." That was the moment that changed everything for me. The transition I was facing continued to challenge me in every sphere of my life. However, the revelation of the process called transition revolutionized my perspective of that stretch of my journey. My trepidation turned to optimism. I was not sure where that trek was going to take me, but I knew it was some place good.

If you are like millions of others, you would describe yourself as being in a place where some area of your life has "ended" and you know you cannot return to it, and your next season has "started" but you have not yet arrived in it. Your right foot is on your "present" while your left foot is moving toward your "future." Part of you is still in "today" while another part of you is stepping into your "tomorrow."

The philosopher Buckminster Fuller said, "Everyone is born a genius, but the process of living de-geniuses them."[1] Would you agree that God is a genius? Of course He is a genius, at a minimum. That being the case, it would be fair to say that God said, "I am going to make a genius *just like me* called man" (see Genesis 1:26). So, everyone is born a genius, but the process of living has a way of de-geniusing you. Transition is the journey back to your genius state. Transition's purpose is to re-genius you.

Most people find themselves perplexed by the many changes that life throws at them. Quite often they find themselves asking, "What in the world is going on," as they are blindsided by some unexpected change—or series of changes that life throws at them. Without exception each person longs for an accurate interpretation of the meaning behind life's sudden turns. The purpose of this book is to alleviate the shroud of confusion surrounding life's interruptions, abrupt changes and difficult surprises, and give empowering perspectives

CONTENTS

CHAPTER ONE

YOU ARE IN TRANSITION

"Just when I think I have learned the way to live, life changes.[1]"
Hugh Prather

In professional basketball the decade of the 1980's belonged to the Los Angeles Lakers. They dominated the game of basketball because of their mastery of a strategy that left their opponents gasping for breath. In the game of basketball possession of the ball changes hands from one team to another hundreds of times during the game. When your team gets the ball from the other team and forges ahead it's called TRANSITION. During that era most teams were progressing nonchalantly through transition with the aim of setting up an offensive play on their side of the basketball court. Not the Los Angeles Lakers of the 1980's. They used transition as their strategy to blow by their opponents before their rival could prepare a defense against them. It worked! Not only did this strategy elevate them above the entire league, but they looked great in the process. They were dubbed "The Showtime Lakers."

The Lakers dominated the game of basketball because of their mastery of transition. They went to the National Basketball Association (NBA) Finals eight out of the ten years in the '80's, and won the NBA Championship five out of the eight years.[2] All of this because of their proficiency and command of transition.

In 1998 I found myself in a period of isolation triggered by my decision to leave "where I was at" without being sure about "where I was going." It was a leave "here" on my way to "there" move. However, I did not know where "there" was. What I did know was, the current season had ended and I knew I could not return to it, and the next season had started but I had not yet arrived in it. I thought I had made a decision to leave a group of people—a decision to leave a system. What I did not know was that I was stepping into an apparent minefield that resulted in an overhaul of my "world-view," an alteration of my "self-view," a reconstruction of my "God-view," and a renovation of my marriage. I was catapulted into the most significant transition of my life. Since that time I have been keenly aware of this thing called transition.

It became clear that life is a series of transitions, and your ability to master transition is the key to you mastering the human experience. On the flip side, your inability to understand and master transition is a prescription for stagnation and potential mental disarray.

The greater your understanding of transition, and the more complete your fluency of it, the greater power it will have in your life. Comprehension of transition will help bring calm and clarity to many of the movements that life will take you through. Let's explore this thing called transition.

Somebody got up one morning and started getting ready for work. Everything seemed normal. They ventured into their normal routine—showered, got dressed, listened to a portion of the morning news on TV, and headed off to work. They made their normal stop at the coffee shop and ordered the usual. They used the commute to help mentally prepare themselves for the day ahead of them. The job they are headed to not only provides ample income but also offers interaction with co-workers who keep the job interesting. The opportunity for advancement is an added bonus. This is an employment situation that they can see themselves staying in until retirement. However, before the end of the day, without any warning, they are called in and told they are being laid off. They just lost their job. One day they were gainfully employed—the next day they are unemployed and trying to wrap their brain around what just happened.

For someone else, the marriage was going good and then things begin to unravel. They never saw it coming. They are suddenly entering unchartered waters—a marriage that is falling apart. They had taken their vows seriously—especially the "'til death do us part" portion. The uncertainty of their relationship has created pressure cooker like tension. They find themselves screaming and yelling in an effort to bring their spouse to his senses, until they realized that debating their position only further alienated their spouse. They sought counsel—both informal (from their friends) and more formally (from a Marriage Counselor). They worried, cried, prayed, hoped, and even tried to change. They did everything they could to hold it together, but it did not work. Now they are facing divorce. They cannot believe it. Just the shock of this eminent conclusion causes their head to spin, at times producing dizziness. It was not supposed to happen. Now, the person who knows all their secrets and flaws is a potential enemy. Plus, they never planned on being single again at this stage of their life.

There is also the individual who did not lose their job, but the realization that they are in a "dead end job" suddenly hit them like a ton of bricks. They realized that in order for them to experience any significant advancement they will have to make a career change. Although that was not the plan, it turned out to be the reality. The thought alone of a career change at this point in their life is enough to produce obvious distress. They are asking themselves a litany of questions. What marketable skills do I have? What steps do I take to explore viable options available to me? Who am I connected to that can steer me in the right direction? What classes will I need to take to help position me for the most feasible opportunities? How do I manage the stress that has moved in and is camping out on my chest?

Then there is the person who has a couple of friends who have started acting "funny" towards her. The friends have not expressed what is influencing the sudden change of their behavior. It is becoming quite obvious that something has changed. The tone of the relationship is totally somber. The flow that was the hallmark of the friendship has disappeared. Although there is a "pink elephant in the room," when confronted about the change of the tone of the relationship, her friends only brush it off as if everything is kosher. The emotional cost associated with trying to maintain the relationships is escalating. Having to resort to pure speculation as to the cause of this mystery is inflating the psychological toll. Really good friendships seem to be becoming rarer. The possibility of losing a set of friends at this point in this person's life is not taken lightly.

Next, consider the person who had not been feeling well for some time. They finally went to the doctor, articulated their symptoms and had a series of tests run. Their Doctor suspected it could be one of two concerns. It took three weeks for the test results to come back. They went for their follow-up visit. The Doctor walked in the room with a stoic look on her face. She disclosed the outcome of the tests as gently as she possibly could. One of the tests came back positive for one of the diseases that the Doctor suspected. Now, they are facing a battle for their health. An entire lifestyle change that includes dietary adjustments and restrictions, a daily medicine regimen, an exercise routine, along with frequent testing at the Doctor's office, has been prescribed as necessary for managing this disease.

Then you have the young person who recently progressed through their teenage years. It suddenly dawned on them that they are not a kid any longer. They are shocked at how quickly they arrived at this point in their life. Everything in their life is saying, "It is time to grow up." They have come to grips with the reality that they are no longer a "child." Although they longed for the day that they could move out of their parent's home, the reality of the responsibilities associated with taking care of themselves has awakened them like a cold shower. The thought of having to maintain an income to cover the cost of rent, utilities, furniture, food, entertainment, a car, car insurance, gas, car maintenance, clothes, and-the-like, is causing them to want that proverbial train to stop, let them get off, and re-board the train they once road while living with their mother and father.

These are all examples of individuals who have found themselves in the throes of transition. Just about anyone you speak to nowadays is in some level of transition in some area of their life. What is transition? I would like to offer some distinct definitions that I trust will expand your comprehension of transition.

TRANSITION IS WHEN ONE SEASON OF YOUR LIFE ABRUPTLY ENDS AND YOU ARE FORCED TO ENTER A NEW SEASON

Life comes at you fast. It presents interesting and unexpected scenarios. The first definition of transition is, transition is when one season of your life abruptly ends and you are forced to enter a new season. The term "season" is used very broadly here. A season is a period of time accompanied by purpose, power, and provision—or a lack thereof. The end of a season can be represented by a multitude of things. It could be the loss of a loved-one. When you lose a loved-one the change happens in a moment. You may get a phone call that someone close to you is gone. The change is instant but it will take time to get accustomed to the reality of what life will be like without the loved-one. The mental and emotional process of learning how to live without the physical presence of your beloved is the transition.

It could be the process of going from being a college student to being a college graduate, from being single to being married, from being childless to having a new baby, or from working for many years to entering retirement. It could be walking through the process of a friendship falling apart, a marriage dissolving, or a separation from a group of people that you were always close to. It could be a geographical move to a new city, or a close family relationship crumbling. Transition is when a change unexpectedly interrupts your world and forces you to respond to it. Something swiftly ends, constraining you to face it. Ready or not, here it comes.

TRANSITION IS THOSE SEEMINGLY INSECURE AND UNPREDICTABLE TIMES IN YOUR LIFE WHEN YOU ARE NOT SURE WHERE YOU ARE GOING OR WHAT'S NEXT

You are familiar with your present, but you do not have the details of your future because you have never lived in it. The routine of your current season gives you a sense of normalcy and a level of assurance about what a day should be like during this chapter of your life. However, when some unexpected life change breaks in on you and knocks the hinge off the door of your life, uncertainty immediately walks through the doorway. The "life shift" triggers transition. The second definition of transition that I would like to establish is, transition is those seemingly insecure and unpredictable times in your life when you are not sure where you are going or what's next. You may not be certain of your next move; however, you are certain that you are not going back to the place where you were. The reality that you are "not going back" could be the result of a conscious decision you made or the result of the place you once knew not even being an available option anymore. You know you are "leaving" but you are not certain about "where you are going." The interruption of the routine and normalcy can easily create a level of insecurity and unpredictability.

If one of the key relationships of your life fell apart in your last season, it is likely to produce skepticism about new relationships in your next season. If you experienced someone in a position of authority over you using manipulation, employing fear and intimidation, or exercising power control and abuse of authority, your sensitivity to and discernment of those in authority in your next chapter will be at an all-time heightened alert.

Oftentimes, when in transition you are not quite sure who you are connected to and for how long. The experiences of your past season awaken a new standard of discernment of people during the next stretch of your life. Your old season gives you the motivation and your new season gives you the freedom and power to institute new guidelines for allowing someone into your space. Just because someone new says, "We need to get together," does not mean you get your calendar out and schedule a lunch date. You quickly learn to respond with, "Let me get back with you on that." A response like that gives you time to consult with your discernment to see if this relationship is worth pursuing. Your discernment is at its peak when you are walking out of a dysfunctional season to a season of stability and clarity. When in transition you will hopefully come to realize that you must translate what you gained from your "past experiences" into your "present reality." This new phase has not come for a repeat performance of your last chapter.

When you are experiencing transition, you will have left your present, but not yet arrived in your future. You will have a strong sense of motion from one level on the way to the next. It would be fair to say you will be between two levels. If I had a glass of water in one hand and an empty glass in the other hand, and begin pouring the water into the empty glass, at one point the water would not be in either glass. It would not be where it was, neither would it be where it is going. It would be between levels. That is what transition customarily feels like. You feel like you are in the middle of somewhere. However, just because it "feels" insecure and unpredictable does not mean it "is" insecure and unpredictable. The sense of instability is a normal response to entering unchartered territory. It simply "seems" unstable. The operative word in our second definition of transition is "seemingly." When all is said and done what seemed to be unstable terrain will likely lead you to a very stable place.

TRANSITION IS WHEN GOD DISQUALIFIES YOU FROM YOUR PRESENT IN FAVOR OF YOUR FUTURE

If you are in a relationship with God He gets involved with the course of events in your life. What you think is your decision to leave a season might actually be God's decision that the season is over. It could appear that a person or a group of people are rejecting you when all the while a season is rejecting you. Your season might be kicking you out. It is plausible that you have been in a period for far too long and you are being graduated to your next era. Your destiny has a way of powerfully pulling you into it.

One of the best ways to get promoted in any arena is to

become overqualified for your current position. When God sees that you are over qualified for your "present" He will promote you to your "future." The bible addresses supernatural promotion by saying, "For promotion cometh neither from the east, nor from the west, nor from the south. But God is the judge: he putteth down one, and setteth up another (Psalm 75:6-7, KJV). If God decides to promote you—you're promoted. The third definition of transition is, transition is when God disqualifies you from your present in favor of your future. If you are in transition and it is scary, just hold on—it could be the hand of God that is disqualifying you from your present. But, it is always in favor of your future.

TRANSITION IS WHEN GOD FORCES YOU OFF THE SHORES OF EGYPT, INTO THE RED SEA, HEADED FOR YOUR PROMISED LAND

The children of Israel spent 430 years in Egypt as slaves (see Exodus 12:40). God delivered them from their Egyptian captors. Then, a few chapters later we read the account of the Egyptians changing their mind and re-pursuing the children of Israel to re-enslave them (see Exodus 14:8). The Egyptian army caught up with the children of Israel where they had set up camp—near the Red Sea. God gave the Israeli leader the escape route. The route was "forward" (see Exodus 14:15).

Egypt represents bondage. It represents limit. The transition that you are experiencing could mean that God is kicking you out of bondage and kicking you out of limit. Before you begin to celebrate I must forewarn you that your first step out of slavery may feel like you have stepped into a minefield. You see, the direction that God pointed the children of Israel to when their former captors closed in on them was a direct path to the Red Sea. Their deliverance from bondage was like being offered a proposition that on the surface seems beneficial, but becomes apparent that the outcome is going to be tragic. It is sort of like walking out of a bad season into an even worse one—walking out of oppression into an ocean. On the surface the Red Sea seemed to be an unfavorable option, but turned out to be an ingenious move. The waters that they thought were going to drown them ended up swallowing their enemies instead (see Exodus 14:28-29). God may have the "waters" that you are facing to serve as a defense for you instead of an opponent against you. The "waters" are not going to drown you. They are only going to wash away the things that cannot go into Canaan with you.

In the bible, water is often representative of the Spirit. In other words, in transition you are leaving the flesh and walking into the Spirit. You are leaving the limits of the knowledge and reasoning of man and tapping into the unlimited knowledge base of God. The revelation is this—when you are in transition, do not consult with flesh (man); consult with God. That does not mean eliminate wise counsel, it means take your transition into the presence of God and seek His wisdom, even on what counsel you will entertain.

So, the fourth definition for transition is this—transition is when God forces you off the shores of Egypt, into the Red Sea, headed for your promised land. The process may feel fatal—it might appear final. But God has a land of promise in His sight that requires a washing away of the things that will abort the benefits of your new land. Welcome to the journey to that place. Welcome to transition!

ADDITIONAL POWER POINTS
- Transition is the bridge on which you travel to get to "the other side." The "other side" is a good place—a "God place."

- The "other side" only comes in view when you embrace the process that God is requiring you to go through to get there.
- God would never speak of delivering you from bondage without having a Canaan Land to replace it with.
- Transition is sometimes like taking a subway. It is an underground passage that at times is dark and enduring. "Dark travels" lead to "bright destinations."
- Transition is your power word for your current season.
- In transition God gets your "heart involved" where in previous seasons only your "head was involved."
- God loves you too much to let everything stay the same so He allows things to become scrambled so He can rearrange things.

CHAPTER TWO
THE MIRAGE CALLED CRISIS

"You're going to go through tough times – that's life. But I say,
"Nothing happens to you, it happens for you." See the positive in
negative events.¹" Joel Osteen

In the book of Mark we see where Jesus ordered his disciples
to get in a boat and go to the other side of the Sea (see Mark
6:45). It turned out that He sent them right into a storm.
They ended up having to contend with unruly winds. The
boat that they were traveling in was battered by boisterous
waves. They were forced into a fight with a whirlwind. When
you leave the shore of "where you are at" in favor of "where
you are going," it is likely that you will encounter a storm.

In Mark's account of this incident he writes, "Then He
(speaking of Jesus) saw them straining at rowing, for the
wind was against them. Now about the fourth watch of the
night He came to them, walking on the sea, and would have
passed them by" (Mark 6:48). The last six words of that verse,
"...*and would have passed them by*," indicates that although
Jesus saw his disciples in what appeared to be extreme crisis,
He had no plans of stopping to assist them. He planned on
continuing His journey without stopping, but was spotted
by his disciples. Why would Jesus purposefully ignore His
devotees while they are in a crisis, especially when He has
a first-hand view of the difficulty? I contend that the crisis
must have served some divine purpose. Consider this—can

you ever learn to stop a storm in your life without ever having one to appear?

Interestingly, prior to directing His disciples to get in that boat, Jesus had just demonstrated the ability to exceed the laws of nature. His disciples had suggested that Jesus order the crowd that had gathered to disperse and go and get themselves something to eat. Jesus told His disciples that was unnecessary. He then demonstrated that you can tap into power from heaven to supersede something that is happening on earth. He fed a multitude of people with five loaves of bread and two fish. Directly after that Jesus directed His disciples to get in the boat and journey to Bethsaida. I believe that Jesus purposefully sent His disciples into a storm. I suspect that Jesus wanted to give his disciples the opportunity to put into practice what He had just demonstrated—the ability to override natural things by tapping into the supernatural.

GOD TRUSTS THAT YOU ARE GOING TO TRANSLATE YOUR "GOD EXPERIENCE" INTO YOUR "STORM EXPERIENCE"

Once Jesus caused the vehement wind to cease, the following observation was made of the disciples, "For they had not understood about the loaves..." (Mark 6:52). In other words, they did not relate their recent supernatural experience (*of feeding many with a few loaves*) to their present battle. What Jesus demonstrates "for you" He expects to see demonstrated "in you." He trusts that you are going to translate your "God-experience" into your "storm-experience."

What appeared to be a storm that "threatened their life" was meant to be an exercise that "advanced their life." People often say, "God is in control." Well of course God is in control of the things that He is in control of. The question for us is can we control the things that He has given us the ability to

14

take control of? That can only be answered by being faced with something that is threatening the peace and progress of your life's journey. The storm that the disciples found themselves in the middle of was an opponent for them to practice their newly granted power on.

IT'S CONCEIVABLE THAT CRISIS IS A "FRIEND" INSTEAD OF A "FOE"

Muhammad Ali, known as Cassius Clay at the time, may still be considered a "good fighter" instead of "The Greatest," had he not faced the then Heavyweight Champion Sonny Liston. Two years earlier Sonny Liston had smashed reigning champion Floyd Patterson in just over two minutes into the fight, to claim the throne. Although Clay was given almost no chance of winning the fight he ended up defeating Sonny Liston, becoming the new Heavy Weight Champion, and going on to be commonly known as "The Greatest." Did the boxing match "make" him great or "reveal" the greatness that was already resident within? Is it possible that the battle that has presented itself has arrived to reveal the greatness that is within you? With that in mind, it is conceivable that the crisis at hand is a "friend" instead of a "foe."

If you are in the process of advancing from one level to another, you are in movement. Between levels is frequented by trouble. Between levels is what is known as transition. The Apostle Paul wrote, "For a great and effective door has opened to me, and *there are* many adversaries" (I Corinthians 16:9). Opportunities are accompanied by opposition. You have to train yourself to think, "If opposition is present then opportunity must be nearby." On the surface, opposition feels like the end. It feels threatening. It can seem like demotion. Pastor Joel Brooks, Jr., teaches, "On your way to your destiny you are going to see three things—persecution, a cross, and then a resurrection."

CRISIS IS A UNIVERSITY

Crisis frequently shows up at the first sign of transition. Transition is triggered by sudden change. Change and crisis tend to go hand-in-hand. Crisis seems to arrive at the same time that change does. Crisis is synonymous with trouble—difficulty and distress. It is when you reach an impasse. Your progress has come to a halt because none of the available options seem feasible. Perplexity. Crisis is disorder, but "disorder" is necessary for "new order." God often uses the things that have gotten "messed up" as a reason to come in and get everything "cleaned up."

Crisis is a university—a literal educational institution designed for information and instruction. It uncovers where you were unguarded. It notifies you about weak structures that you thought could hold you up under the scrutiny of adversity, but turned out to be unreliable. It advises you about your lack of judgment. It teaches you the areas that you can never "go to sleep on" again. It informs you of the disciplines that you will be required to put in place in order to not repeat the current tragedy. It infuses you with an alertness that you never would have gained without the dilemma you faced. It schools you in the art of preparedness for future trouble. Crisis exposes your vulnerabilities so you can shore up your fragile areas in time for the next challenge. It trains you to put safeguards in place for the future that were not in place in the past.

Crisis is also a great tool for revealing strengths. It is great at reminding you about durability that you possess that you had not been required to display in a long time. Educational institutions not only test your knowledge and abilities, they also exhibit them. Not only does crisis remind you of your qualities of tenacity and courage, but it skillfully reveals character that you were not aware you possessed. Trouble is masterful at bringing to the surface your ability to respond, think on your feet, make great decisions under pressure, endure scrutiny, and keep your cool in the face of extreme tension.

I was recently faced with what I will call a $48,640 challenge. To overcome this predicament I was required to answer dozens-and-dozens of questions with documentation to support each answer. In some instances I was asked the same question on different occasions and was obligated to provide an answer with accompanying documentation each time, as if the question was never asked before. Several of the demands were unreasonable. To add to the challenging nature of the process, the system was not set up for my answers to go directly to the persons making the final determination. My contact person was a "go between" that had the task of conveying the decision makers' requests to me, and communicating my position to the decision makers. Interestingly, I noticed that my contact person was not nearly as pleasant in the morning as she was in the afternoon. So, I felt it necessary to strategically time my calls to match her anticipated mood.

I wrote over a dozen letters. I was scrutinized in areas I never imaged I would ever need to answer for. I was ignored, run through a human-size ball of red tape, asked to re-submit documents that they lost, and required to produce documents for which there was no template. In addition, I stood in line at the county court house for my turn to be probed by a deputy, and then passed through a metal detector, all to simply get access to a required death certificate. After three weeks of haggling I had submitted a stack of documents and letters of explanation that measured four inches in height.

Although this process was ridiculous and extremely frustrating, I noticed that I was able to respond to any request for anything asked of me within one hour, no matter how difficult the request. I was never stumped, even when it initially appeared unlikely that I could meet a particular demand. This opportunity to exercise my ability to respond quickly, concisely, and with a high quality, demonstrated that I had advanced several levels over the past few years. It revealed that I was quicker and sharper than ever before. The activity necessitated me to tap into my optimum creativity. I sailed through the process, calling on my ultimate patience and forbearance. I proved that my highest nature was available to me whenever needed. The unpleasant and taxing circumstance turned out to be an opportunity to display my mastery. I had a front-row seat, observing my distinction of being lightning fast on my feet, decisive, in command, calm, and creative. What seemed like it was meant to impede, outwit, and dishearten me, turned out to only refresh my memory of the fact that I can counter any complication thrown at me with quickness, creativity, and quality. After all, that is what I am all about.

Transition has many faces. Transition allows "what was" to fizzle so it can be replaced with "what's supposed to be." You see, God is so creative that He creates an entirely different day each morning. In plain English, your today is not supposed to look like your yesterday, and your tomorrow should be an even greater surprise. That is why (I believe) God allows scenarios of change in your life—to create movement and momentum so you do not miss the element of surprise He has stored in your future. If you stay in your current situation of frustration and stagnation, so too will your thinking. Where your mind goes your body will follow. The thinking associated with a world of stagnation and frustration will keep you a prisoner in a zone of unfulfillment.

IN TRANSITION "COOPERATION" RESULTS IN "ELEVATION"

You may be in a season of wondering why things have been a bit crazy in your life. It is likely that God is squeezing out of you what was allowable on the prior level but is not tolerated on the next level. Sometimes God will seemingly pick you out of the crowd and appear to allow everybody to get away with certain things but you. He will give you a set of disciplinary requirements that others would not even consider. He may tell you things like He wants you to get up each morning and pray before the sun rises. He may require you to avoid certain people and connect with others who you would not consider to be "your type." He may compel you to study when everyone else is playing. He might obligate you to work out every-other-day, throw away those donuts, monitor your calls, "zip your lips" and open your ears. The next guy might be allowed to light up and smoke a pack of cigarettes a day and nothing happen to him, and you try to take a puff and go into a coughing fit. If you are one who cooperates with God, there are times where He may put you on a program of discipline and regiment that makes boot camp look like a cake walk. When God does that you must cooperate with what He is doing. He may have you in transition. In transition, "cooperation" results in "elevation." Your cooperation with the disciplines God is requiring is the gateway to the next level you have been seeking.

There are cases when your next level has been waiting for you for years, but it will not let you in until you meet the qualification requirements. The demands you have been experiencing could be part of the prerequisites necessary for entry into your next era. That would mean that the turbulence you have been experiencing is proof that you are in line for promotion.

GOD DOES NOT WANT YOU TO WALK INTO FREEDOM AND STILL HAVE THE TENTACLES OF BONDAGE IN YOU

The enemy does not care if you enter your Promised Land, as long as you take some of the irritants in there with you, so Canaan still feels like Egypt. God knows it is possible that you can enter Canaan and not enjoy the milk and honey when you get there because you are distracted by baggage that you brought with you. In the fifteenth chapter of John Jesus said, "...and every *branch* that bears fruit He prunes, that it may bear more fruit (John 15:2b). When God is involved in your transition you can bet on the process involving some pruning. Pruning is the process of cutting away the dead branches or stems to increase growth and productivity. Sometimes you do not break into your next level of life because you have not displayed the qualities that the people on the next level demonstrate. In other cases individuals make it to the next level when they have not met the requirements. It is almost as if an imposter made it through the filter of the next level. However, one of the worst places to be is on a level that you do not have the qualities and character to support. You will either stick out like a sore thumb or be deported back to the station in life that you have been accredited for. In order to legitimately go to the next level there has to be a cutting away of that which is keeping you where you are at. It is what Jesus is referring to when He says "pruning." God does not want you to walk into freedom and still have the tentacles of bondage in you, so He uses transition to cut away and cut off the things that are hindering your progress into your destiny.

It is painful to have something cut off of you. That is what is known as crisis. It can be excruciating. In order for you to have "more," you have to have "less" first. You have to lose what can prove to be detrimental to the next chapter and phase of your life. The "pain of the present" is for the purpose of producing the "pleasure of your future."

The agitation and discomfort of this crisis should be irritating enough to motivate you to do everything in your power to assure nothing like this ever happens again. Bitter pills do not go down easy. Neither are they easily forgotten. If a set of personal decisions produced the pain you are experiencing, the realization that your lack of judgment was to blame makes it even worse. To have a repeat failure would be even more excruciating, given the fact that your experience should have taught you how to avoid this in the future.

IF YOU PUT ALL YOUR FOCUS ON THE "MESS" YOU WILL MISS THE "MESSAGE"

When the relationship between objects and the horizon becomes distorted as a result of extreme heat on the surface of the ground, a mirage is formed. A mirage is an optical illusion. It gives the visual impression of one thing that turns out not to be as it appears. The most common mirage is when it looks as if there are pools of water sitting on a hot road.

When the relationship between the crisis you are facing and the positive possibilities that it can produce becomes distorted, a mirage is formed. The mirage is an optical illusion that this trouble has come to "destroy you" when in reality it will be used to "promote you." It gives the optical illusion of a "peril" that in the end is going to be for your "profit." The function of the mirage is to sabotage your journey. If you put all of your focus on the "mess" you will miss the "message." If you keep a cool head and tap into the process, you are destined to experience the betterment hidden in the cloud of the dilemma.

God does not waste any part of you—even your flaws. Your "issues" are likely to get you in hot water at some point. The best way to deal with your issues is for your issues to deal with you. When who you are produces a troubling predicament, you have no one to implicate but yourself. If you have any level of maturity you will cite yourself as the responsible party and begin to take corrective action. The benefit of the mess that you created is that you feel the pain of what your weakness produced. The pain should provide the impetus to initiate the self-reexamination and alteration. Messes produced by your defects can trigger a new quality of "self-editing." The by-product of the crisis can be an upgraded version of you. Maybe now you are a person that no longer "says it" just because you "think it." Perhaps the new-and-improved you discloses your flaw to someone close to you and asks them to point out (to you) when they see you reverting to your "lower self." It may be that whenever you are tempted to judge someone, instead of speaking about them, you now pray for them.

What appears on the surface to be meant to "bury you" can be used to "elevate you." Just because it "looks bad" does not mean it is "for bad." Some of the best things that come from you will be when something unpleasant is happening to you. What you "name" you "keep." During the creation process the bible says, "Out of the ground the LORD God formed every beast of the field and every bird of the air, and brought *them* to Adam to see what he would call them. And whatever Adam called each living creature, that *was* its name" (Genesis 2:19). That gigantic, trunk swinging, peanut eating animal is still called "elephant" to this day. All because Adam gave it that name years ago. Why not rename your next crisis "mirage."

ADDITIONAL POWER POINTS

- Never let a crisis enter your life without knowing what it deposited in your life during its stint in your journey.
- The current crisis may turn out to be the rungs on the ladder that takes you to the top. You may end up getting to walk "on" what tried to walk "over" you.
- Do not get stuck on what the trouble did "to you," wait to see what it does "for you." It may take the "future" to unfold what your "past" crisis produced "in" you.
- Just because God did not order your current crisis does not mean He can't use it to produce something masterful.
- One "wrong thing" can awaken a lot of "right things."
- Let your crisis take you to school. Take good notes. Make sure that the "agitation" leads to a "graduation."

CHAPTER THREE
The Contrast of Change and Transition

"The only way to make sense out of change is to plunge into it, move with it, and join the dance.[1]" Alan Watts

Although change and transition are in the same family, there are some very telling differences between the two. Change and transition are excellent partners. Nevertheless, even though they work very well together, they are not the same thing.

Consider the young man who asks God to give him a wife. While he has the wisdom to ask for God's input in the process of finding his soul mate, he does not have the foresight to ask for the patience and clarity of mind that will be required to enjoy his new wife while trying to grasp her idiosyncrasies.

For instance, he grew up with a lively exchange of conversation around the dinner table, while she was brought up with the understanding that you are not supposed to talk while eating dinner. Their first few dinner experiences as a married couple are awkward. She's wondering why he is talking so much and he is trying to figure out why she has put herself on mute. It turns out that this is only one of a handful of discoveries about the women of his dreams that (to put it nicely) seems a bit weird. The excitement, passion, and pure love for his new bride add enough weight on the other side of the scale for these quirks not to be considered deal breakers. However, he has quickly been awakened to the fact that he has to call on several new skills—forbearance, acceptance, patience, and understanding—in order to successfully fulfill his role as *husband*.

When God gave him his wife, God permitted the change the young man was seeking, knowing all the while that if the youngster does not allow the "change" to produce a "transition," he will be in trouble. In other words, you can get married and still remain single in mentality. Getting married is "change"—embracing what it takes to become a successful husband is "transition." Saying "I do" at the altar is the initiation of the change. However, the introduction of the transition takes place when you embrace saying "I do" when you are bombarded by your inclination to say, "I don't" multiple times because something your spouse is doing conflicts with your standard way of operating.

Many people are looking for change. Change is on the radar of most people because the winds of change have been blowing so profusely for the last several years. We have been struck with harsh economic changes, especially after the Nine-Eleven tragedy. Many have been blindsided by loss of employment resulting from corporate cutbacks. Institutions, organizations, as well as individuals, have been forced to reassess their spending in an effort to guard against extinction and future financial meltdown.

Change is everywhere. You are likely to have experienced your favorite item suddenly vanishing from the menu of the quick serve establishment that you frequent. What was once a popular customer choice may no longer be cost effective for the restaurant because of an exorbitant increase in their cost to stock the item. As a consequence they may discontinue offering it with no meaningful explanation to those, without whose support, the establishment would not be there. You have probably encountered a litany of examples of product, service, and system changes that seem to inconvenience the person for whom they are meant to provide a convenience. Systemic pressure is driving "cut backs" that lead to the eventuality of the end user being "cut off." We are seeing knee-jerk reactions just about everywhere spurred by fear of loss. These reactions result in change. Change seems to be omnipresent.

"EXTERNAL CHANGE" MUST PRODUCE AN "INTERNAL REORIENTATION"

Many changes "happen to you" and several other changes are "chosen by you." You can choose to end a relationship, change car insurance companies, move to a new city, disassociate from an organization you are a part of, or retire early. That's change. However, if the "external change" does not produce an "internal reorientation," transition has not been triggered. Transition will place a demand on your emotional, psychological, and spiritual engagement. It will require of you to make the internal adjustments necessary to merge the change you are facing into the person you know yourself to be. Many changes are taking place without the redirection of one's heart. As a result, many people are exerting a great deal of energy moving from "here" to there, and when the dust settles, ending up right back "here." Moving around but ending up right back in the same situation.

THE DIFFERENCE BETWEEN CHANGE AND TRANSITION

What is the difference between change and transition? Change typically happens in time—an incident, an initiative, a decision, an act, an event, a tragedy. Nine-Eleven happens, your wife gets pregnant, you lose someone close to you, or a meaningful relationship falls apart. A change occurs. Change is external—transition is internal. Change happens outside of you—transition occurs inside of you when you embrace God's perspective of the change that just happened. Transition is the journey of getting your heart and your head wrapped around God's perspective regarding the change that you are experiencing. Not every change results in a transition. Many changes result in people just moving around and ending up in the same place. It is important to embrace the journey triggered by the change. That way, the impact of the change is that its outgrowth will be a transition.[2]

One of the most common misconceptions is that because something is ending it means it is "the end." In transition, the beginning actually starts with the ending. Transition starts when something ends. It could be the end of a marriage or the end of a way of thinking. Actually, the end of a particular way of thinking means you have entered transition. One of the most powerful things you can do is be clear about what is ending. That is imperative in order to experience a successful transition. You must recognize what is ending (detach), allow time for old structures to be taken apart (dismantle), and restructure (remantle) for the future. **Detach**, **Dismantle**, and **Remantle**.

DETACH

Consider the individual who had been a part of a particular organization for a number of years. It was woven into the very fabric of her day-to-day life. Many aspects of her involvement gave her a sense of family. If she needed emotional support, someone from the organization was there to lend her such support. When she needed help with her children she could rely on an informal father-figure to step in and provide quality mentorship and a masculine perspective that brought balance to her single-parenting position. She was a part of a rare "tribe" that was so prominent in her life that she, in great part, defined who she was by her affiliation with that group.

In time, as she matured, many of her personal views became clearer to her. She slowly began to notice that some of her internal convictions collided with the group that she was entwined in. It began to create some psychological conflict. The clearer she became about her personal beliefs the more blaring the contrast with the group's beliefs became. There was never any doubt as to how much she loved the individuals within the organization; however, doubt started to creep in about how accurate her involvement in this group represented who she was as an individual. After all, a great part of her personal identity was entangled in the identity of this organization.

She started noticing that she would be in organizational meetings physically but separated from them emotionally. It finally became clear to her that she could not remain engaged with the group without violating her internal convictions. She eventually recognized that this relationship had to come to an end.

Recognition of what is ending involves acknowledging that "it's over," "this has reached its expiration," "there's no more life here," "this is the end to the relationship as we know it." When the ending is acknowledged and accepted, you have entered the detachment phase. You should define what's no more and understand that transition has come knocking.

Again, some endings are chosen "by you" and other endings happen "to you." Some are so blatant that they announce to you, "It's over." Be it the passing of a loved-one, the loss of a job, or a spouse leaving for good. Recognition of what is ending is the beginning stage of transition. That is when detachment happens. Keep in mind that your ending will naturally produce a new beginning. In order to have a "new beginning"; however, you have to have clear vision of an "old ending."

DISMANTLE

The onset of the detachment phase will naturally trigger a dismantling of old infrastructures. The framework within which you functioned prior to the detachment will probably serve no further purpose. The young lady who was struggling with how her identity matched the organization's, eventually formally announced to the group that she would be "moving on." Now, the weekly meetings that kept her bond strong with her fellow group members were eliminated. Her required loyalty to its leaders was discarded. The sense of accomplishment when the organization was recognized in the community for something noble vanished. Her sense of duty to represent the institution, that sometimes was more compelling than her convictions to represent her individuality, quickly faded. The architecture that was the footing for her attachment to that organization was being dismantled.

You must allow time for the emotions associated with the detachment to flush themselves out. If the attachment was strong enough, it might feel much like grieving the loss of someone close to you passing away. Give yourself time for the old infrastructures to be taken apart. Dismantling must take place. You have to let go of what will no longer be useful and get rid of what will no longer be necessary. Dismantling has a vital role. "Dismantling" is to allow room for "remantling."

REMANTLE

The word remantle is not in the English dictionary. As far as I can determine it is not considered a word. I would like to offer it as a new word. Remantle relates to reassembling the parts of your life that were dismantled (or disassembled) resulting from detachment (something ending). It is the recreating and reconstruction of your identity, patterns, and assumptions. Remantling is not taking what got disassembled and putting it back together the way it "was," it is putting it back together the way it "needs to be." It is to align you with God's original intent for your divine destiny.

So much of your identity can be attached to what you used to be a part of, who you used to associate with, and what your title and position used to be, that you can lose your identity during detachment. Remantling relates to the restructuring of your identity and patterns. Detaching and dismantling will "open you up" when you welcome what they represent. Once you are open you are empowered to remain open. During this phase you must be open to letting go of what people identified you by. You may have formerly been known as such-and-such's wife, or the head of that department, or a member of that prominent church. Suddenly your detachment strips that identity from you. What on the surface seems like a loss, could be an opportunity for you to find new, wonderful ways to identify yourself. Remantling affords you the opportunity to look inside and begin to become familiar with who you are, independent of your association with and attachment to any system, institution, organization, or title.

If you really want to make a change "stick" you must go through the process of transition. You must adjust your thinking, your assumptions, your perspective, and your heart, to incorporate the change into your world. It is the fool proof way to make a meaningful change become permanent. Keep in mind that transition is a process—it's a journey. There are some basic components of a journey. I would say, distance covered, mode of transportation, element of mystery, and a sense of fulfillment. Let's give thought to these.

DISTANCE COVERED
To meet the definition of a journey, a significant amount of distance should be covered. It takes time to go a far distance. The further your journey takes you the more perspective

you should gain. Most of the time transition is a journey of tremendous distance covered. You go beyond short travels "of your head" and enter long and winding travels "into your heart." You find things in there that you know you must discard and you embrace new realities that you know you must employ, in order for the journey to be all that it was destined to be.

MODE OF TRANSPORTATION
Your choice of how you cover ground while on a journey is significant. It determines how much flexibility you have with pace. It determines how quickly or slowly you will arrive. Although speed may not be an important factor if one of your objectives is to take in the scenery and experience the cultural amenities. Your choice of transportation determines if the journey will be a smooth venture or a bumpy one. It even determines if you will make it from point A to point B. "Transition" is actually "transportation." It is how you get from where you are in life to where you are supposed to be. It is how you get from one level to the next. If you fail to buy-in to the process of transition it is likely that you will remain in the same place mentally, emotionally, financially, socially, and spiritually.

ELEMENT OF MYSTERY
A legitimate journey will have an element of mystery associated with it. That is part of the intrigue—to not know what's around the corner of every turn. The component of discovering and experiencing the unknown is a significant part of the allure of a journey. When you are in transition there are a lot of twists and turns. Never make up answers to explain away a mystery. If you knew all the answers you would not need to consult the one who does. Embrace what's around the corner—having the expectation that it is something good. God wants you to have a sense of enjoyment even without a sense of answers.

A SENSE OF FULFILLMENT

What makes a journey most significant is the sense of fulfillment associated with it. Being able to articulate what you experienced and how it reshaped the way you see things and relate to people, makes the journey worthwhile. If you are fortunate enough to gain understanding of the fact that you have global significance—that your presence in the world is necessary—you will experience an even deeper level of fulfillment. You will come out of transition different than you went in. It may take a lifetime to unpeel all of the layers that were added on to you during transition.

Here's further perspective on the contrast of change and transition:

Change	**Transition**
Change is external.	Transition is internal.
Change is viewed with eyes.	Transition is viewed with vision.
Change happens "to" you.	Transition happens "in" you.
Change involves your head.	Transition involves your heart.
Change is an external occurrence.	Transition is an internal experience.
Change happens in an instant.	Transition happens over time.
Change alters the scenery.	Transition alters how you look at scenery.
Change happens often.	Transition happens more seldom.
Change can make you brace yourself.	Transition is something you need to embrace, yourself.
Change affects you.	Transition "in"fects you.
Change results in change.	Transition results in transformation.
Change can be good or bad.	Transition is good and God.
Change is a decision.	Transition is a dissection.
Change is well-known.	Transition is not commonly known.
Change is an event.	Transition is an "in" vent.

ADDITIONAL POWER POINTS

- Never let a major change come without embracing the transition that should accompany it.
- The purpose of the *external* change is to produce the *internal* transition. The external *heat* reaches the internal *heart*.
- Transition is triggered by sudden change. When sudden change comes you better change. Whoever changes first will become the leader—either you, or the circumstance.
- You must be willing to change something "in you" before you expect to see change "outside of you."
- External "progress" results from internal "process."

CHAPTER FOUR
THE AGITATION OF YOUR PRESENT

"The unknown is not always out to get you. Sometimes, the unknown
is seeking to bless you.[1]" Undrai Fizer, Ph.D.

Your present is for a short period of time—your future is
forever. Your present represents today—your future represents
tomorrow. Your present will last for a short period of time
and your future will last for a long time. It's easy to see why
God places more emphasis on your future. The point you
have made it to today has already been established. It's your
tomorrow that requires attention.

WHEN GOD SHOWS YOU YOUR FUTURE IT
SPOILS YOU TO YOUR PRESENT

You were created for movement. Everything God made
was made for more, movement, and multiplication. The first
commandment God gave to man was, "Be fruitful (that's
be more), and multiply (that's multiplication), and replenish
the earth;" *the implied verb is "go"* (that's movement). When
God's mantra is "go" and your experience says "stay," He will
support scenarios of change to create movement from your
present into your destiny. So what God will do is show you
your future to birth dissatisfaction with your present. When
God shows you (as a young person working at the local fast
food franchise) a vision of you owning it, you start to feel
the tension created by the gap between where you are and

35

where you hope to be in the future. You used to not mind sweeping. But now the future owner inside you suddenly becomes frustrated with sweeping the floor. You continue to sweep but with more excellence because you now have a sense of how your future employees are going to need to approach this task. However, from the moment God places ownership in your heart, sweeping will never be the same. It's all because when God shows you your future it spoils you to your present.

When you are vision oriented you are always in the future while trying to manage your present. That creates tension. The greater the gap between where you currently are and where you are going to be, the greater the tension you will experience. Tension is created when you hear things like "You're a millionaire," but you barely had enough gas in your car to make it to the inspirational meeting that confirmed your destiny of financial security. In transition your mind will try to make your destiny look like "if," when it's really a matter of "when."[1] The challenge is this—God usually shows you big things while in small places.

A number of years ago God placed a strong desire in our heart to build a custom home. At that time my wife, my three daughters, and I, were living in a rented home with one bathroom. Four females sharing one bathroom required a considerable amount of patience, forbearance and understanding. The conflict was that our desire for the custom home was not born at the same time that the resources to build it were. There was a considerable gap between those two worlds. However, we began touring custom homes for sale in the area on a regular basis in spite of our present reality. We attended the local Parade of Homes each year. The Parade of Homes is a showcase of new homes. We set up files that contained ideas for each area of our future home. After three years of spending time in custom designed homes, gathering and filing dozens of ideas, and aiming our giving toward the harvest of our own custom designed home, the gap between our present and our future narrowed. The initial tension between our present and our future that started out extreme eventually became manageable. At some point the custom designed home environment that originally seemed foreign began to feel normal. And, the resources necessary to build begin to find their way to us. Three years and six months from the day the desire was birthed, we moved into our custom designed home. Although we had never lived in a home like that, the environment felt very familiar. We had successfully managed the tension created by the gap between our dream and our reality by preparing for and practicing living in our dream. You can pray for things and wait for them to materialize, or you can prepare for the things you are praying for. Your preparing is the initiator of the answer to the prayer you prayed.

One of the greatest things about your present is, if you don't like today it will be over in a few hours. If you don't like your current experience, God has placed a thing called tomorrow on a twenty-four hour repeat pattern. A new day is as close as tomorrow. There was a point in history where the Children of Israel were experiencing a famine. The situation was bad. Elisha, the prophet declared, "Tomorrow about this time...it's going to be plenty and it's going to be affordable..." (II Kings 7:1 *paraphrased*). Elisha had gotten tired of famine, lack, desolation, barrenness and hunger. He declared that within twenty-four hours we are going from "famine-to-fabulosity," and from "hunger-to-harvest." He went on to state with power and authority that, "Tomorrow, at about this time, things are going to change!" Tomorrow can be represented by two things. It could mean the end of the calendar day and the beginning of the next. Or, it could mean the end of a season. You have heard the phrase, "It's a new day." When people use that terminology they are not referring to the end of a twenty-four hour period. They are saying, "I'm no longer tolerating my present situation. I'm birthing a new season." The beginning of that new season constitutes your "tomorrow." You can decide that this current season of failure and frustration is over and initiate the start of your tomorrow.

Have you come to a place where the provision has dried up? Maybe the pleasure has ceased. Have you remained in a setting where the purpose (the very reason for being there) has become tainted? Have you awakened to a season where you can no longer articulate the meaning behind your actions? Are you changing while everything around you is staying the same? Are you watching the clock in desperation for a break in the action, or hoping it reads, "Quitting time?" Do you habitually show up "there" physically while you travel to "someplace else" mentally? Do you secretly wish the whole organization would dissolve so you no longer have to be a part of it? That way you are relieved of ever having to jump ship and explain why. Have you become an imposter within the organization? You give the impression of a team player in public, when in private you are actually an opponent. Have you finally mastered the art of playing the script that they wrote for you when everything in you says, "This is not who you are?" Have you become the clone they pressured you into becoming in the unwritten rules, only to realize you are better at being a clone than you are at being you?

THE PAIN OF YOUR PRESENT SHOULD BE ENOUGH MOTIVATION TO PURSUE YOUR FUTURE

There's no reason for a thirsty person to stay where there's no more water. If you are thirsty for "it" and it's not "there," go find "it." If you hate going "there" then quit torturing

yourself. Figure out how to find a job you love; a group of
people you love; a place you love; an environment you love.
If this level is not producing enough for you, then elevate
to another level. The pain of your present should be enough
motivation to pursue your future. I am not necessarily saying
you should just walk out today; rather, you should start
planning your steps out today.

I recently observed two young people quit jobs that they
hated without having another position lined up. They
"walked out" without having planned their "steps out." I
would not recommend that, unless you have the financial
security to support yourself while you are looking to land
your next position. I believe that your current agitation (be
it on your job or within a group or circle that you run in)
should be the fuel that motivates your next move. Perhaps
you are an entrepreneur "in your heart" but an employee
"in your daily experience." Maybe the entrepreneur in you
hates going to your current job. Why not keep your job,
take an hour a day after work, and additional hours on the
weekend, to strategize and put your business plan together.
What if you launched your business and worked it on a part-
time basis until the income from your business supersedes
the income from your job? You would have the benefit of
multiple streams of income in the process, along with the
security of your current job until the business proves to be
viable.

WHAT GOD DOES "IN" YOU CAN CAUSE YOUR ENVIRONMENT TO REJECT YOU

There are times where God may take you through a process
of leaving a group of people that you love. God starts the
process by developing something in you that collides with
what the group embodies. The more you embrace the
new thing that God is doing in you the less it aligns with

your current tribe. Your new development can eventually disqualify you from the group. In essence God disqualifies you from your "present" in favor of your "future." Your preferred surroundings end up rejecting you. You may experience the people that you love being used as the agitators that produce an environment in which you can no longer stay. There are some places that you will never "get to" until you leave some other places that you have "come to." There are certain places that God wants to promote you to, that you would never come to, because you would never think of leaving the people that you are so close to. So God allows the flaws of those you love to go unmanaged. Their dysfunction creates a toxic environment that eventually you can no longer bear. So you are forced to say, "I love you but I have to go. It's not that I don't love you, it's that I can't be with you for now. I must go." I heard Marvin Winans say, "You oughta' thank God for those people who acted up. You would not have moved out if it wasn't for them."

Places also matter. There are times when your destiny is "there" but you are "here." So God deposits "there" in your heart. You may discover a sudden desire to move to a new geographical location. I am not referring to looking for a new city to be the answer to settling your unsettled soul. I do not mean when you have no direction and you think a new city is going to give you new direction. If you are moving to Georgia because it's an "up-and-coming-location," without you already being an "up-and-coming person," you are going to be disappointed in Georgia. What I am referring to is when God is placing a geographical move in your heart to connect you with your destiny. But, if you are moving because you expect a "new city" to give you a "new life" without you having become a "new you," you will be shocked at how much living in Texas feels just like living in the state you just moved from.

A physical move should be the manifestation of the fact that something "in" you already left the building *so to speak*. It should be a reflection of the fact that you have grown up mentally. You stopped processing what others do "to" you in a way that gives them power "over" you. A physical move should really be a manifestation of the fact that you already left the building emotionally. You cried before over a particular thing. You acted like a baby and stayed in frustration. But you finally realized that resorting to that emotion was not producing the results you wanted. So you are not crying any more over that. A physical move should be a manifestation of the fact that you already left the building in maturity. You are finally mature enough to be able to say, "I was wrong," "That was my fault," "I apologize," "I will rectify the situation." In other words, you no longer live in the prison of projecting what's wrong with you off on other people. Once you have left spiritually, mentally, emotionally, and in maturity, then your physical move becomes legitimate. A physical move should be the outgrowth of a deeper expansion.

Now there are times when the thrill leaves but the purpose is still in tack. Your sense of responsibility keeps you in place although the fun has dissolved. Sometimes God requires you to remain in place for the present so what you are a part of does not unravel. You are needed and necessary right where you are. The newness of anything will eventually wear off. However, some assignments are permanent. You have to discern what you are connected to and for how long. You have to discern if God is requiring you to stay or if it was God that created the scenario of agitation that resulted in the desire to leave. Could it be that God wants to take you through a radical transition of change that triggers a change in everyone else around you? What if God is choosing you as the "first born among many" to walk in new levels of integrity and truth? Maybe your "transformation" resulting from your "transition" is so radical that everyone in your circle or organization becomes infected? Is it conceivable that God might place you in a transition of change and have you "stay" instead of "leave?"

ADDITIONAL POWER POINTS

- Your present isn't permanent. It is the floor on which you walk "today" to get to your "tomorrow."
- The present agitation is to provide motivation for your elevation.
- There are times when God dislikes your present more than you do. So He allows the puzzle pieces of your life to spill out of the box so He can come along and put each piece where it fits, to create the picture of your next chapter.
- You cannot get to your tomorrow without leaving your today anyway. The quicker you can get "over it" the quicker it will "be over."
- Sometimes you will never know the importance of boundaries until someone crosses one of yours.
- Could it be that the resistance you are experiencing is "divine" and not "demonic?"

CHAPTER FIVE
HIDDEN FOR A SEASON

"Those things which I am saying now may be obscure, yet they will be made clearer in their proper place.[1]" Nicolaus Copernicus

Some transitions are triggered by God leading you to leave without telling you where to go. God famously told Abraham, "Get out of your country, from your family and from your father's house, to a land that I *will* show you," ... *not a land that I "have" shown you* (Genesis 12:1). Heading in a direction for which you have not received a route can produce a sensation of wandering. Being led to an unnamed place, detached from those with whom you have never ventured without, is likely to induce a sense of disconnection. Could it be that God is intentionally leading you into a hidden place? When in transition, it is common for you to be led into hiding. It's like, "Where God is leading you, He's hiding you." Have you ever experienced being hidden for a season? Maybe you are smack dab in the middle of a season of hiding in this moment.

If you are being hidden, it could feel like you have been temporarily deactivated—literally unplugged, for a period of time. Perhaps the factory of your life has been shut down temporarily for retooling. Retooling speaks to the reality that a new product or a new result can only be generated by rearranging and replacing the tools required to produce it. Retooling can be a slow and expensive process. However, when God has arranged the overhaul, the new product of your life will exhibit a pleasant merit that your personal factory never yielded in the past.

In transition the enemy wants you to think you are a few emotions away from falling apart. You have one foot on your present while the other one is trying to break into your future. You have one foot on your today while the other one is stepping into your tomorrow. Its like, "Am I in my present or am I in my future? My today seems like it's over but my tomorrow does not seem to have started yet." Due to you only having one foot on the ground, your apparent lack of footing can easily cause you to feel open to attack. Your "uncertainty" is what feeds your "vulnerability." It's not that you are weak, it's that you are uncertain of your next step.

Perhaps you have been in a black-out season. You have been hidden. You cry when you are alone, but your tears roll smoothly down your face and hit the hard ridged surface of the ground unnoticed. You cry, but your cry has not reached the ears of those who care enough to do something. In transition, do not take your tears to mean you are feeble and faint, but that you are uninhibited and unreserved. You are open. The tears that flow from your eyes are a reflection of what is being released from your heart. Tears tell. They tell God what your heart does not have the ability to articulate. The tears of this season will teach in your next season.

Maybe you have been speaking, but your voice has not reached the ears of those who can validate what you are saying. You feel like you have something worthwhile to say but the audience that would be impacted does not show up. Do not resist the fact that you have been put on mute temporarily. In transition, sometimes silence is louder than speaking because "wrong words" will always do more damage than "no words."

Most people speak from the place of the most blaring obstacle they are facing at the present time. For example, if a person is walking through the valley of a divorce, the damage typically reveals itself in their conversations—any conversation about any topic. You could be discussing the latest news about how a franchise basketball star exercised his option in free agency, and signed with a different team. It is plausible that your current pain will remind you that you too are being separated or abandoned (just like the basketball star's former team). Just about every conversation you have with anyone gives you a platform to speak from your place of pain and detachment. When your distress is "top of mind" it can easily come to the "top of your conversations." If you feel damaged, do not advertise it. Put yourself on mute. Part of the purpose of a season of hiding is to protect you from yourself—from the damage you might cause from speaking from an injured place. It is hard to speak stable words when you are unstable. The bible says, "So then, my beloved brethren, let every man be swift to hear, slow to speak, slow to wrath" (James 1:19). We spend about 90 percent of the time talking and 10 percent of the time listening. The wisdom of this verse is implying it should be the opposite...90 percent of the time listening and 10 percent talking.

Perhaps your greatest strength in this season is having something to say and not saying it. The ability to have strength and not put it on display is more powerful than displaying it. This is a season to allow your display of discipline to be more visible than your display of strength. Your apparent black-out period is a season for listening, discerning, sensing, and downloading what is being disseminated from the throne room of heaven. By the time "they" are ready to hear what you have to say you will be speaking from a loaded position. The power behind your words will have a potency that can only be produced by the solitude of your season of hiding. When you come out of this season your words will have the quality of a slow cooked meal in preference to a two-minute microwaved meal.

You may feel like you have enough wisdom to make an impact in the lives of others, along with the motivation to do so. Maybe you have hidden desires to make a difference, but the opportunities to make a difference are hiding from you. You are qualified to teach but *for some reason* it's not time to teach. Maybe you have the "credentials" but God wants you to have the "providential." He wants to confer on you His power and endorsement. Are you present, but it seems that nobody sees you? Do you feel invisible? Could it possibly be that God is hiding you for a season? Could it be that you are under reconstruction?

God told the prophet Elijah, "Get away from here and turn eastward, and hide..." (I Kings 17:3). It turned out that where God "hid him" is where God "fed him." The entire verse reads, "Get away from here and turn eastward, and hide by the Brook Cherith, which flows into the Jordan." The next verse says, "And it will be that you shall drink from the brook, and I have commanded the ravens to feed you there." Verse 6 says, "The ravens brought him bread and meat in the morning, and bread and meat in the evening; and he drank from the brook." Although he was hidden, his provision never considered him lost. Where God "hides you" He "feeds you." Your place of hiding is where God makes right everything that is wrong; cleans up everything that is messed up; straightens out everything that is crooked; fixes everything that is broken; replaces everything that is lost; and God restores everything that was stolen!

USE SILENCE TO CREATE SOUND

Some of the most amazing times that I have had in prayer is when I went to pray and said nothing. I did not come to talk, but rather to listen. One of the highest forms of prayer is "listening." Sensing the promptings of God while in transition, is a form of prayer. "Should I move, or stand still?" "Is this a season of researching or a season of launching?" Discerning the cues of God is a part of the communicative process called prayer. Is the absence of God's voice a clue to the fact that you have asked a question that He has already answered? Sometimes the loudest thing God says is nothing. Even God's silence creates words. Sometimes God not answering is the answer. It may mean the path you are taking is already on heaven's GPS. Perhaps heaven does not want to throw you off. God's silence sets the tone for His speaking. If He is of a few words, when He does talk it's definitely going to be something worth hearing. Do not sweat it if God is not talking much. All it takes is Him saying "one thing" to wipe out years of Him not saying "anything." "One word" can compensate for a history of "no words." His silence could be relaying, "You are on the right track—you are taking the right direction."

Sometimes the loudest sound you can make is silence. You're screaming, "I'm in position to receive impartation." If two people are talking at the same time it is very likely that someone is going to miss what the other person is saying. Do not talk when God is talking. Listen. If God has you hidden for a season expect periods of silence. God may be revolutionizing your environment to make it conducive for you hearing what the noise of life has been drowning out. He could be conditioning your spirit to hear the sound that silence creates.

Whenever someone is restoring a classic car they do it in private. The restoration process can be ugly and gets messy. The restoration process is typically done in a garage— behind closed doors. Nobody sees it—it's hidden. The restorer is wise to hide the process because people will judge your future based on your present. God never gives your present a vote when determining your destiny. Once the classic car is restored, the owner brings it out of hiding and shows it off. The Psalmist David said, "For in the time of trouble He shall hide me in His pavilion; in the secret place of His tabernacle He shall hide me; He shall set me high upon a rock" (Psalms 27:5). Notice that he repeats "He shall hide me." God is doubling the fact that He will hide you in seasons of "trouble." Transition is often accompanied by trouble. Chapter two highlights the fact that trouble (crisis) is a mirage. It's something that the enemy uses to bury you, but God turns it into the very ground you are going to stand on in your next season.

WHILE IN THE WILDERNESS DON'T GO INTO THE CITY

Stay hidden for a season. You could be in the wilderness for a season so you cannot be found by the people that celebrate your stagnation. The next time they see you they will not recognize you. Your life will have a whole new scent to it. The bible said of Jesus, "Though He was a Son, *yet* He learned obedience by the things which He suffered" (James 5:8). Jesus learned obedience in the wilderness. Pain *sometimes* is a privilege. It's a signal that something is out of order. Pain teaches you what to avoid in the future. Pain tells you what never to let happen again. Matthew 4:1 says, "Then Jesus was led up by the Spirit into the wilderness..." Wildernesses are sometimes Spirit-led places. It's where you realize what's ending, discover your new identity, and receive your supernatural power for the next era of your life. While in the wilderness don't go into the city. Remain hidden, especially if God is the one who initiates the season of obscurity.

In seasons of hiding it's not just quiet "times" with God—its entire "seasons of quiet" with God. Seasons of hiding are also for revealing to you what's hidden inside you that will abort your entry into the next era of your life. It is very likely that God will include an up-close-and-personal examination of your character in your season of hiding. Mark 4:34(b) states, "And when they were alone, He explained all things to His disciples." God typically does not let the public in on his personal revelations of your character issues that need to be cleaned up. He does it while you are alone.

GOD IS MORE COMMITTED TO WHERE HE'S TAKING YOU THAN HE IS CONCERNED ABOUT THE DISCOMFORT YOU'RE EXPERIENCING ON THE RIDE THERE

Heartbreak, disappointment, the loss of a friendship, sickness, and failure, trigger seasons of aloneness. These things have a way of emptying us out. When we are "poured out" God can begin to "pour in." There are flaws in you that will not prevent you from entering your new season, but are destined to spoil the amenities when you get there. So God catches you when you are dumbfounded by some catastrophe. When you are unable to speak He can take the stage. It is then that He can expound upon the things that you have ignored that must be corrected. You may be shocked by what God expounds on about you when He has you alone. God's replay wheel may show clips of you that reveal deceit, lies, theft, jealousy, lust, envy, and rebellion. When this occurs, do not resist, deflect, blame or make excuses. When God is performing "heart surgery" you must cooperate. If God uncovers it He believes you have the capacity to face it and accept it. Never come face-to-face with the truth without accepting the truth. What God "reveals" He can "kill." God's revelation of your defects is proof that your destiny is important enough for God not to allow some character deficiency to prevent you from reaching your highest dimension. God is more committed to where He's taking you than He is concerned about the discomfort you're experiencing on the ride there.

IN TRANSITION, THE GIANT THAT APPEARS TO BE BIG IN YOUR MIND TYPICALLY ENDS UP BEING LITTLE IN YOUR EXPERIENCE

During your season of hiding God understands that if you were to land right now it would be too messy. It would be too ugly to put you on display right now so God is supernaturally hiding you. People look at you but seemingly do not see you. If you were to land right now it would seem too crazy for you to be taken serious by those you are called to impact. Keep in mind, seasons of hiding are just that—seasons. They are temporary. "Hidden" does not mean "forgotten." At some point God is going to open the garage door of your life. And your voice will be heard, your tears will begin to teach, and your desire to help will be welcomed. At some point "the classic" will have been restored and put on display. Let God hide you for a season. He's simply seasoning you in the hiding. Just hold tight—because if you are in transition it's not the proof of opposition but the proof of promotion.[2] The giant that appears to be big in your mind will typically end up being little in your experience. You will come out of this black-out period and the light will shine on you again.

ADDITIONAL POWER POINTS
- There's only one thing left when you're hidden from everything else—God. When everything else is veiled then you can see Him.
- In a season of hiding and being recalibrated by God, silence may be the last stage. It's God's way of communicating, "There's nothing left to say."
- There are things about you that you must discover that you would never consider unless it was done in a classroom

of one. "Private instruction" leads to "public graduation."

- If God has you in the dark, you are not studying to find your way "out"—but to find your way "in." It's when you discover what's "in you" that you understand why that shocking behavior came forth "from you."
- In your season of hiding you don't have to hide—that is, if He's hiding you.
- You will know that God has you on a special program when He's orchestrating everything. His voice is louder than normal; His instructions are clearer than usual; and there are signposts at every turn.
- What you hear amongst the crowd must be examined when alone with God. Oswald Chambers said, "We listen to many things in classes, but they are not an exposition to us yet. They will be when God gets us alone over them.[3]"
- When God has you in stillness do not move. It's what God produces "in" you that determines what proceeds "from" you.

CHAPTER SIX
UNCOVERING HIDDEN FACTS ABOUT TRANSITION

"Its not only moving that creates new starting points. Sometimes all it takes is a subtle shift in perspective, an opening of the mind, an intentional pause and reset, or a new route to start to see new options and new possibilities.[1]" Kristin Armstrong

There is a proverb that says, "*It is* the glory of God to conceal a matter, but the glory of kings *is* to search out a matter" (Proverbs 25:2). The proverb says, "But the glory of kings is to search…" If you see yourself as a king you should find yourself searching for hidden truths. Revelation (the unveiling of hidden truth) is for Kings who find glory in searching for and finding truths and realities that will change their life, and the lives of those around them forever. God's "hiding" produces man's "seeking." Man's "seeking" results in man's "discovery."

There are some amazing facts about transition that sometimes are veiled. The expression, "You can't see the forest for the trees" comes to mind. It implies that you can get so involved in the details of a problem that you can't see the entire situation as a whole. When that happens you can potentially miss a divine moment hidden in a difficult situation. When you find yourself in transition it is advisable to search for the hidden empowering benefits shrouded by the chaos. Keep in mind that you may not be able to fully realize all the value you received in the transition until years after you have walked through it.

I would like to expand your perspective and enlighten your imagination of transition by outlining Seven Facts About Transition.

1. Many of life's transitions are scheduled for you.
The Psalmist David said, "The Steps of a good man are ordered by the Lord..." (Psalms 37:23a). When you are walking with God and He is orchestrating your journey, transition just shows up. Transition is triggered by things like an unexpected significant change, a seasonal change based on reaching a certain age, someone important leaving your life, or someone significant entering your life. The manner in which transition shows up in your life is not the determining factor of who is behind it.

Just ask Joseph in the bible, whose brothers had thrown him in a pit, pulled him out, sold him to some Arabs, who sold him to an Egyptian named Potiphar. Potiphar happened to be a member of the personal staff of Pharaoh, the king of Egypt. Through his relationship with Potiphar and a series of other significant events, Joseph was eventually appointed as Governor of Egypt, where he orchestrated the only available supply of food in several surrounding countries. This led to his brothers being forced to travel to the only available food source, where they encountered the one they thought they had gotten rid of forever. Joseph's articulation of this story has become one of the most popular biblical quotes in modern Christianity. He concluded, "What you meant for evil God meant for good" (Genesis 50:20 paraphrased). God manipulated man's evil plans and transformed them into God's purpose. Joseph became extremely wealthy and ended up feeding his brothers in famine. His transition to the "palace" started with a stay in the "pit."

Chapter 6

EVEN IF YOU "FALL" IT DOES NOT HAVE TO BE "FATAL"

I am not in the camp of those who blame God for the bad things that happen in your life. I believe that God is not capable of doing anything bad. However, I am convinced that God does not waste any (what we would call "bad") experiences. Many of our experiences are the result of decisions that we made, some are the result of the natural consequences of evil in the world, others are a consequence of where, or to whom we were born, and many are the outcome of the environment we find ourselves in. Obviously God is not shocked by "any of it," and can—and does—work with "all of it." So, God is not ordering the bad things that happen to you, but is orchestrating the good things that come from it. Even if you "fall" it does not have to be "fatal," especially when God is masterminding the transition.

2. You can birth transition in your life by deciding to reject your current level in favor of a higher one.

There are times in your life where you need to make a decision to go to the next level. Your experience is telling you that being on this level is outdated. One of the most powerful things you can do is come to a conclusion about something. To decide means to draw the line. It means you are defining what you will no longer allow and what you will begin to welcome going forward. Rejection of your current level initiates the transition to a higher one. The Apostle Paul profoundly stated, "Brethren, I do not count myself to have apprehended; but one thing I do, forgetting those things which are behind and reaching forward to those things which are ahead" (Philippians 3:13).

WHAT YOU ARE WILLING TO "REJECT" DETERMINES WHAT GOD CAN "INJECT"

You are not required to wait for transition to show up. If you see value in transition you can birth it by a quality decision to tell the level that you're on, "Goodbye." Your level is the place to which you have come in life that you operate from. One of the main purposes of transition is to get you from one level to the next. You can initiate the process by simply deciding that this level has reached its expiration date, this season is elapsed, and this foolishness must be terminated. What you are willing to "reject" determines what God can "inject." Some of the greatest "additions" to your life will come when you have made some "subtractions."

3. Habits of the first level don't work at the next level.

I believe that God gives you your "life" but allows you to create your "world." In other words, God gives you the liberty to determine what the experience of your life is like. Your decisions, perspective, attitude, actions, and reactions, all help paint the picture of what life is like for you. Another vital determiner of what your life experience is like is the habits you employ. A great life is created by great habits—excellent practices patterns and routines. What you do regularly— what you do "as a rule" is a predictor of your life results.

Every level that you can operate on has a code of acceptable and expected conduct. If you honor the code of conduct you will be allowed to remain. If you dishonor the code of behavior you are likely to be demoted from that level. In order to advance to a higher level of life you have to elevate your patterns. You have to advance your habits. Procrastination may not be detrimental on the current level of life that you are operating on, but could be a devastating habit on the next level. Questionable integrity might go undetected and seem insignificant at the place in life you might find yourself today. However, there are levels of life that you cannot even enter without meeting the qualification of operating at the highest level of integrity. Winging it is acceptable in some operating environments and not tolerated as you advance to more significant settings.

Assess your patterns. Study the things that you do habitually—good and bad. It is likely that a faulty habit is producing opposing results in some area of your life. See if you can trace the dysfunction in your life to a pattern, or set of patterns that are damaging. This time do not blame the devil. Every time you blame the devil you resurrect and empower someone who was put to death. The Apostle Paul wrote, "Having disarmed principalities and powers, He made a public spectacle of them, triumphing over them in it" (Colossians 2:15). Paul is colorfully stating that Jesus stripped every oppressive spiritual entity of their fraudulent authority and made it public for everyone to see.

IN TRANSITION YOUR SEASON WILL CHANGE ONLY AS FAST A YOUR DECISION TO CHANGE A HABIT THAT'S BEEN STIFLING YOUR GROWTH

So, define the habits that produced your dysfunction. Begin the battle to kill every dysfunctional habit. In the context of our discussion, when I say "bad habits," the traditional bad habits of smoking, over eating, or using foul-language, don't come to mind. However, being late, procrastinating, moving slow, ignoring what's important because it stretches you, all come to my attention. In transition your season will change only as fast as your decision to change a habit that's been stifling your growth. Quite simply, when you change what you do, your results change. It's time to replace an old "poor" habit with a "great" new habit.

If you go into your next season with the same patterns as your old season you will likely be disappointed by your inability to thrive in what should be a promotion. The higher the level you reach, the higher level of discipline that will be required. Study the patterns and practices of the level you are trying to break into—compare notes with your current patterns and see what needs to be adjusted, abandoned, or adopted.

4. Some people at the first level don't work at the next level.
When you are breaking into higher levels of thinking and behaving, it will require the involvement of other aspects of your being. Your conversation—the things that you normally talk about, your language—your choice of words, your etiquette—proper and customary conduct, will likely be required to have an upgrade. It is difficult to change your choice of words when you are in the company of those who use the language you are seeking to abandon. On the other hand, it is much easier to embrace proper etiquette when everyone around you is adhering to the protocol.

Some of the people you currently associate with have no intentions of changing the way they operate. If they are not willing to acquaint themselves with the code of ethics of the new level you are pushing towards, they are only going to clash with the new mindset that you are embracing. If they are not willing to go where you are going, in new ways of thinking and behaving, they probably do not qualify to walk with you in this season. You do not necessarily have to kick them out of your life; you may need to simply move them from your inner circle to your outer circle. You can start bringing your lunch instead of going to lunch. Elect to go out less and stay in more. Go shopping by yourself, or connect with someone on the level that you are advancing to. Diplomatic avoidance sends a gentle signal that you are graciously withdrawing.

There are other cases where you have to make the cut-and-dry decision to take a break from certain individuals. Your destiny is making a blaring call for you, and you know you cannot risk your advancement by allowing an obvious distraction to accompany you. Not only are you known by the people you hang with, but you are also known by the people you avoid.

5. Successful transition requires your willingness to change.
Change is one of the most prevalent things in our lives these days. Do not be fooled into thinking that because you have experienced a great deal of change, you have changed. Alteration can be happening all "around you" without it influencing a change "in you."

YOU WILL NEVER RECOGNIZE A BETTER APPROACH WHEN YOU ARE CONVINCED THAT THERE ARE NOT ANY AVAILABLE

When one of my daughters became a young adult I was blown away by the stark difference in her attitude, demeanor, focus, perspective, and the spirit she carried. As her teenage years were ending, so were her negative attitude and combative nature. She began to display a calm, focused, mature disposition. I finally asked her why her middle and high-school experience was not nearly as pleasant as her young adult years. Her reply was, "I was living closed back then—now I'm living open." Amazing! She recognized that she was "living closed." When your heart is shut, wonderful opportunities for self-development can present themselves to you and you not even recognize them. You will never recognize a better approach when you are convinced that there is not one available.

Never become so convinced that the way you are approaching things is so right that you totally block out any and all alternative ways of operating. One of the beautiful things about being in transition is that new and creative perspectives present themselves to you. If you "live open," as my daughter would say, you are moving forward with a willingness to change. An open heart is one that expresses, "There could be more effective, appropriate, and fulfilling avenues than the ones I am currently taking."

Being in transition is about cooperating with your divine destiny. Having a cooperative spirit means you are open to the fact that you need to change. Some of the most pleasant people to be around are those who have embraced the fact that they need to change. In order to experience a successful transition you have to be open to taking a different path, slowing down, speeding up, overlooking the trivial, becoming more aware of the miniscule, or having a complete overhaul of your world view. One, or several of these, may be new and exciting challenges presented to you by the transition you are experiencing. If you are not "open" to personal change you may remain in a "closed" and confined existence.

When you think about making personal changes consider an alternative route than the one most people take. Instead of going right to some external thing that you need to stop doing—like being critical of people—go inside and assess what inside you fuels the need to put other people down. Do not try to use willpower to stop talking about people. Address the "internal issue" that results in the "external behavior." Maybe a deficiency in your own behavior pushes you to bring others down as a way of leveling the playing field—causing others to appear deficient like you. Focus on your "internal issues" that result in your "external conduct." Focus on the internals—your motives, fears, reasoning, and prejudices. As you address the internals and focus on what is influencing them, you will find that you will have a better handle on your issues and inclinations.

The willingness to change is a symbol of humility. It is an admission that you may be wrong in some area of your life. It is an acceptance of the fact that there is more to know, room for growth, and many more options to take than you have discovered.

6. In transition the change you're seeking God to bring might be the one He's seeking you to make.

There are times when we are waiting on God to do something that He is waiting on us to do. You're waiting on God—He's waiting on you. You are looking at Him to see when He is going to move on your behalf, while at the same time He is looking at you to see when you are going to move on your behalf. It could be that this transition has showed up in your life to get you to make a move—to do something that really needs to be done.

Entertainers are great at recognizing those who came before them who paved the way for those coming behind them. There are comedians who came along and addressed certain societal issues comically unlike others before them. There have been musicians that introduced styles of music that were unheard of prior to them. There have even been entertainers that rose up who did not have the looks that the industry says you are supposed to have in order to captivate audiences. When they broke a barrier they opened the gates for all those coming after them who are uniquely gifted, unusual and out-of-box. Likewise, God has said and done some things that paved the way for every human being that walks the face of the earth. He created entryways for us to walk through and disseminated power and authority to enable us to act in our best interest and on behalf of others. The bible uses language like, "But you will receive power...,"

"For I have not given you the spirit of fear, but of power...,"
"But I have given you the power to tread upon serpents
and scorpions, and over all the power of the enemy..." (see
Deuteronomy 8:18, II Timothy 1:7, and Luke 10:19). God
does not want you to expect Him to do the things that He
gave you the ability to do.

Make sure that the change you are seeking God to bring
is not the one He is seeking you to make. Get up and act.
Get moving. Do what you have the power to do. You always
have the power to ask, reach, knock, seek, call, study, and
research. Many times God's power kicks in when you are in
motion. The first thing that God ever said to man was, "Be
fruitful"—be productive. One principal of "the law of first
mentions" is that all the power necessary for future results is
hidden in the "first mention." When you are attentive to the
first thing God ever told us (i.e. be productive), results start
following you.

Jesus said, "Whatever you bind on earth will be bound in
heaven" (see Matthew 18:18). It is as if He is saying, "You do
something first and I will do something next." "You bind (or
forbid) something first, then I'll guarantee it's bound."

Transition requires your involvement. It requires your
thought, personal assessment, open heart, and willingness
to make important and necessary changes. There are times
when it seems like God is not answering our prayers. It
could mean we are asking for something that God already
gave us. Or we could be asking God to do something that
He has already done. If either of those are the case, then the
next move is probably ours to make.

**7. If you are going to be used by God, He will take
you through a multitude of experiences that are
meant more for others than they are for you.**

In II Corinthians 1:4, the Apostle Paul, speaking of Jesus, said, "Who comforts us in all our tribulation, that we may be able to comfort those who are in any trouble, with the comfort with which we ourselves are comforted by God." In some unique way we all are interconnected. Let's say you are in a season where things are going extremely well, but someone you know is in a season where things are going very badly. Is it accurate to say that you are doing great when you are aware that your friend is really struggling? You are compelled by the knowledge of your brother or sister's pain to get involved, even if it is as minuscule as briefly thinking of them and considering their pain. Dr. Martin Luther King, Jr. said, *"I am cognizant of the interrelatedness of all communities and states. I cannot sit idly by in Atlanta and not be concerned about what happens in Birmingham. Injustice anywhere is a threat to justice everywhere. We are caught in an inescapable network of mutuality, tied in a single garment of destiny. Whatever affects one directly affects all indirectly."[2]*

Some of the experiences that you encounter are not meant for you as much as they are meant to make you useful to others. There are experiences that you have that gives you an understanding of what transpires in the heart of others so that you will always have a sensitivity to those individuals. A powerful byproduct of transition is that it will awaken you to what others may be dealing with and inspire you to reach out more powerfully than you have considered in the past.

ADDITIONAL POWER POINTS
* Sometimes the biggest reward you get in a season of seeking answers and clarity is the time you got to spend with God.
* God does not so much hide things "from" us as He does "for" us. He protects the hidden truth until you are ready to receive it.
* Do not expect all the mysteries surrounding your

transition to unfold at the same time. Focus on embracing and enjoying the process.

- What you open your heart to finally has a chance to make its presentation. You might be pleasantly shocked by the slant presented.

CHAPTER SEVEN
Don't Go In a Caterpillar Without Coming Out a Butterfly

"This flesh in which we live is nothing more than a cocoon,
and only when we step out of it do we truly begin to live.'"
Nancy Stephan

When you are in the midst of transition, you are likely to hit a place where you sense there is something inside of you that needs to be released. Something good—something quality. Something that has reached its hour to be revealed. It is conceivable that you will be awakened to the realization that something inside you changed and should be displayed and drawn on by those who can benefit from it. It could even be that this yearning inside of you is what actually triggers the transition you are experiencing. It is common to have the capacity to sense something strong needing to emerge from you without the ability to effectively articulate what it is. However, the fact that you cannot "put your hand on it," does not negate the fact that it is undeniable.

There should be points in your life where you conclude that your "tomorrow results" have to advance beyond your "today experiences." There must come a time when you just know you have to do better. It's as if your destiny becomes dissatisfied with your progress. You feel a sense that you must "step on the gas." There is an internal mandate for you to improve. There is a natural push for you to make headway. You are compelled that next week has to be better than this week. You become determined that next month must be brighter than this month.

For those who have been in church for a long time—there is likely to come a time where you require more than the ritualistic experience of a typical Sunday morning service. Your inner man may begin to ask questions like, "When am I going to "see" the materialization of what I hear them "say" week-after-week-after-week?" "When are the years of "rhetoric" going to show up in my day-to-day 'results'?" "Am I required to live my entire life in the box of the perspective of one person who stands before me and spiritually philosophizes each week?" "Is this Christian experience more than gathering each week for church services?" "How many more years are we going to "talk about doing something" and actually "do what we have been talking about?" The Apostle Paul seemed to have a good feel for this as evidenced by him saying, "For the kingdom of God is not a matter of talk but of power" (I Corinthians 4:20 NIV).

As a child I spent a great deal of time outdoors. As I woke up in the morning the longing to break free from the confining walls of the house was pulsating within me. Stepping outside was like stepping into freedom. I stepped into nature's symphony, filled with the sounds of screeching crickets, chirping birds, and howling winds. I was stimulated by the smell of the moist dirt in the nearby woods, titillated by the aroma of the sap dripping from the nearby maple tree, along with the fragrance of the roses from the rose bush growing up the side of our garage.

Then there was my observation of the many species of insects. I saw countless caterpillars creeping slowly along the ground. I was mesmerized by the soft flying butterflies that filled the air of my neighborhood. Although I surmise that

I was taught as a child that caterpillars eventually become butterflies, I did not make the correlation as I observed each of them in their separate state. It was not until I was an adult that it was really clear to me that the artistic looking butterfly floating through the air with such grace, used to be a funny looking, slow moving caterpillar bound to the ground.

When I observed the caterpillar I was always looking down on the ground, although I would occasionally see one on a tree. When I observed a butterfly I was always looking above the ground, as they used air beneath their flapping wings as leverage to keep them airborne. The caterpillar is limited by the ground. It can only move in the shape of the earth. The butterfly is unrestricted. There is no ground to limit the path of its progress.

Moving From Humanness to Unlimitedness

Man was made by heaven and placed on earth. Every one of us has heaven and earth inside of us. Earth is representative of humanness—with its limitations like the caterpillar. Heaven is representative of the divine—with its unlimitedness like the butterfly. Because the three-dimensional world is physical (you can hear it, see it, touch it, smell it, and taste it), it seems to be more prominent and powerful than the unseen world. No analysis is necessary to determine if the chair you are sitting in is real. It's tangible. It's undeniable. However, it takes effort to refer to something that you cannot see, and consider it to be real. It requires exploration, seeking, analyzing, researching, and ultimately discovery, to tap into the invisible world that controls the visible world.

However, for some individuals something unexplainable and undeniable happens in their life that can only be attributed to "the hand of God." The "unseen world" invades their "seen reality." They get to bypass the process of discovering the unseen world through exploration. No initial seeking was necessary because heaven busted in on them. But most have to go through the process of seeking and discovering the unseen world. Every step you take in the direction of seeking and discovering what is available to you from heaven (the unseen world), is a step away from humanness and limitation.

Transition has a way of igniting a desire to explore possibilities of power available from the unseen world or either triggering a forced entrance of the invisible world into your present reality. I am convinced that one of the overarching purposes of transition is to provoke an appetite for something more potent and powerful than anything you have experienced in the past. I believe that one of transitions objectives is to point you in the direction of God—to awaken you to the Spirit world.

Spirituality seems to be extremely fashionable at the present time. It's almost as if you will not be considered sophisticated if you do not reveal that you are "spiritual," especially if you are a celebrity being interviewed on TV. I am not sure that I know what people mean when they say they are spiritual. I would like to offer that spirituality is the awareness of, and connection to the unseen world, that controls everything in the seen world. The author of the book of Hebrews says it this way, "So that the things which are seen were not made of things which are visible" (Hebrews 11:3b). Spirituality is the understanding and awareness of the reality that the source of all power and rule is from a governmental authority beyond this physical world.

Don't Remain a Mere Human

You must tap into the part of you that has the ability to connect with the supernatural. You are divine. If you came from heaven you fit the definition of "divine" (of, from, or like God). You cannot experience a transition that results in a transformation by tapping solely into human thoughts, human concepts, human ideas, and human strategies. If you refer only to human knowledge, you run the risk of remaining a caterpillar, bound to the lowest place of life— on the ground. Confined to only moving in the shape of the earth. Full of the potential to have a metamorphosis but stuck in humanness.

If you find yourself in transition it is a blaring signal that you are not to remain a mere human. You have to realize that this transition will require you to seek God. It will urge you to consult heaven. Transition will insist that you gain a spiritual perspective of your current position. It will necessitate that you not act without heaven's instructions. Transition will dictate that you seek God's promptings and urgings before you make your next move.

That is what gets you off the ground into the air—from flesh to Spirit—from humanness to the divine. The Apostle Paul wrote, "But we all, with unveiled face, beholding as in a mirror the glory of the Lord (the weight; heaviness; awesomeness; the shine of God) are being transformed into the same image from glory to glory, just as by the Spirit of the Lord" (II Corinthians 3:18). When Paul says, "With unveiled face," that means there is nothing veiling our face. He says we are looking into a mirror, and what we are seeing is the awesomeness of God. The verse goes on to say that we are being transformed into the very thing we are looking at. In other words, the more we look at God the more we become how He is. The more you study how God thinks, acts, and moves, and imitate it, the more you will experience God-like results.

That is your mandate when you are in transition. Get God's perspective on what you are dealing with. Seek heavens counsel. Do not make a move that God is not influencing. That is the way you get elevated above every place that you have ever been in life. The last part of II Corinthians 3.18 concludes that we are transformed into something divine. We metamorphose from caterpillar to butterfly—from a mere human to one who has tapped into his divine nature.

When you are in transition you must turn to the spiritual. If you rely solely on the flesh (humanness) instead of the spirit, you will remain in a crawling position. When you consult the Spirit—the Spirit of God—you leave the ground and become airborne where you are not susceptible to the limitations of an "on your belly" position.

A caterpillar cannot fly. While it is known that a caterpillar cannot fly, it is undeniable that it has everything necessary to fly resident within. It has to go through a process to go from crawling on the ground to flying through the air. It is called a metamorphosis—a literal change of the form or nature of a thing into something completely different.

The transformation of a stubby, crawling caterpillar into an airborne fairy has long fascinated humans. The stages of development from a ground-crawling bug to an air-flying beauty are intriguing. You have The Feeding Stage, The Child Inside, Multiple Stages of Development, and The Metamorphosis. Each stage is a powerful metaphor of the various phases of transition.

THE FEEDING STAGE

During the feeding state the caterpillar is a virtual eating machine—devouring many times its own weight in whatever its chosen food plant might be during its stage as a crawling insect. The caterpillar does this quietly and secretively. Here's the message—the beginning stage of transition is the time to consume as much spiritual nourishment as you can get into your system. Be selective. Seek God regarding what you should consume. You are looking for that which feeds your spirit—your inner man—the core of your being where your decisions, desires, motives, priorities, and thoughts are designed and developed. Like the caterpillar, do it quietly and in private. It is not necessary to broadcast your transition. You are not quite at where you are going. You are in process. You are in transition. Keep it under wraps. During the feeding stage you are being infused with the new framework that will eventually get you off the ground—from a crawling position of mere humanness to a flying position of a divine being.

THE CHILD INSIDE

Inside even the smallest caterpillar that is just hatched from a minuscule egg, there are bundles of cells already primed and destined to become adult features such as antenna, wings, and legs. These bundles of cells are prevented from growing and developing by a constant wash of a juvenile hormone.

The revelation is this—when in transition, in order to "get off the ground" into the air you have to lose the immaturity. You must stop blaming. "Shame" always "blames." Blaming is merely casting the responsibility you are supposed to take, off on to someone else. You have to come to grips with the fact that a wonderful process called transition is being presented to you. Stop being defensive, suspicious of people, and looking for a fight. As long as you refuse to relinquish the immature tactics, that juvenile hormone will continue to roam free and prevent the growth that will be necessary to set you free to fly.

MULTIPLE STAGES OF DEVELOPMENT

When the caterpillar reaches a critical size, a burst of skin-shedding hormone is released. The skin becomes too tight as a result of the fast speed at which the caterpillar is growing.

It causes the caterpillar to shed its skin several times, each time forming a new stage of development.

Here's the message—in transition God walks you through several stages of growth. With each new stage comes new skin. You shed the skin that held you together at the prior level in favor of new skin. It's skin that is not confining. Your skin gets thicker. You no longer care as much about what "they" say about you. You get more pliable skin—you are less rigid, and more flexible. You are open to new and creative possibilities. Your skin is continually upgraded to accommodate the growth you are experiencing.

THE METAMORPHOSIS

In the final caterpillar stage, the bundles of cells have already begun to emerge from their enforced dormancy and started to grow. Juvenile hormones now fall below a threshold and the next skin-shedding hormone surge stimulates the change into a hard case known as a chrysalis (often referred to as a cocoon). The chrysalis protects the butterfly while it is turning into an adult. Fully grown caterpillars attach themselves to a suitable twig or leaf before shedding their outside layer of skin to reveal the chrysalis. Along with the ability to occasionally twitch in response to threats, this shell is what protects the caterpillar while it transforms.

It is during this stage that the caterpillar experiences a metamorphosis. It starts to turn into a butterfly. It starts to look different. Its shape starts to change. It changes quickly. It then turns into a butterfly. An adult butterfly will eventually emerge from the chrysalis where it will wait a few hours for its wings to fill with blood and dry, before flying for the first time.[2]

The revelation is this—when you have relinquished the immaturity and received an onslaught of power, revelation, and heavenly impartation regarding the transition that you are in, you will eventually be promoted in the spirit realm. It is as if heaven acknowledges and endorses that you have successfully gone through the process. In transition, your emphasis should be placed on what happens inside the cocoon. It is a time for focusing on what is being imparted to you in your private moments with God. It is a spiritual transformation that you are accentuating. You are aiming for spiritual elevation.

You must be awakened to the fact that your perspective must be elevated to a level that is higher than the level that the challenge you are facing is on. If you seek answers, solutions, resources, and power, which are "on ground level," you will remain on ground level in your experience. Once you gain insight and discernment from a higher level than your current experience, what used to be your experience automatically gets elevated to that higher level. You will have a new sense of wisdom available to you. Wisdom is the ability to discern what to do. You will have new spiritual instincts that accurately show you what to do in any and every given circumstance.

When you are in transition the caterpillar represents your humanity—the butterfly represents your divinity. Again, divinity is of, from, or like God. When in transition, you have to get in the spirit, and stay in the spirit. In other words, you have to de-emphasize "natural things" and emphasize "spiritual pursuit." You will only go as far as the revelation and impartation at your access. Your transition is your season for seeking spiritual revelation and impartations from God in doses and at levels that you have never approached before. Your access to and infusion of spiritual power is what is going to keep you in a flying position. It will allow you to simply fly above what used to dictate the path you could take, because the spirit realm is always higher than the physical world. As you advance spiritually God promotes you to a new world—a new perspective—a whole new way of operating.

A butterfly's genius and beauty emerges when it loses it chrysalis (its cocoon). The flesh in which you live is your cocoon. Your genius and beauty will emerge when you break out of the limits of your humanness and tap into the spirit.

A butterfly is one of the most elegant works of art found in nature. Their colors are bright, and intense. Their wings appear to be deliberate works of art by a skilled artist. You will see various rich shades of gold, orange, blue, lavender, grey, and purple. The bright colors are often contrasted by darker shades to create the appearance of the finest couture clothing. There are variations of symmetric shapes sprinkled with dots. Like the butterfly's artistic expression, observing and experiencing someone on the other side of a God-orchestrated transition is a thing of beauty. You will observe and experience a more graceful, enlightened, assured, refined, updated, improved, well-informed, and often more delicate individual. Transition has a way of revealing your highest nature—displaying the best that God has put inside of you.

ADDITIONAL POWER POINTS
- God can get you to where you need to be from any place you're currently at.
- There is beauty in you that you are not aware of that will not only enhance the experience of those with whom you interact, but will upgrade your own experience with "you."
- Let your transition unwrap the best of you that is hidden from your current reality.
- God is an artist. He painted your beautiful wings and placed the artwork in your DNA. Many things in life have blocked the view of your wings. Transition is God's

process of peeling back the layers of gunk concealing His artwork.

- The cocoon that's been confining you is proof you have something beautiful inside to fly with.
- What fed you at the prior level will not advance you to your next level. You must eat the food of your next level in order to advance into it.
- Don't go in a caterpillar without coming out a butterfly. Embrace the process—stay in it until it brings you out.

CHAPTER EIGHT
FIVE REASONS WHY TRANSITION IS SO GOOD

"Every exit is an entry somewhere else.[1]" Tom Stoppard

Many times negative things seem to have a much louder voice than positive things. A sensational story about a fatal car accident will get news coverage more quickly than a story of a youngster who became valedictorian of his high school class, despite being raised in the projects by his aunt because he lost both parents to violence. Most people who have complained to the restaurant manager about a server that provided sub-par service have never pulled a manager aside to tout the exceptional service they received by a server. People gossip at work about something they do not like about their boss; however, it is unlikely to hear rumors circulating about how amazing a boss is. There can be a multitude of positive things happening around us that gets very little of our recognition, and one negative thing can come along and get our undivided attention.

It just dawned on me that the reason behind our preoccupation with the negative could have a positive meaning behind it. Could it be that God put an innate expectation in us to assume things are going to go well and be well? Maybe God put in each of us an "internal knower" that presupposes good, and so when we see or experience bad it shocks our system, sending it into investigation mode. Something in us expected good and got surprised to see something bad, forcing us to interrogate the unexpected occurrence. It

77

produces a curiosity about what went wrong. It shows up as a preoccupation with negative news, events, or incidents.

Have you ever thought about how many things have to have gone right for you to be where you are today? There are usually many more positive things to make note of than there are negative. Most of us do not do as good of a job chronicling the positives as we should. Hearing of too many negative things, or actually experiencing an unreasonable amount of them can make you cynical and spoil your expectation. That's why it's important to adjust your perspective on a regular basis. Sometimes the very thing that *on the surface* seems "bad," turns out to mean "good."

There are elements of transition that can be outright unpleasant. Overall though, the mission of transition is to lead to something good. To broaden your perspective, here are Five Reasons Why Transition is Good.

1. The next thing that God is bringing you into is always better than the current thing.

When God made you He put the best that is ever going to come "from you," "inside you." God never starts anything until He finishes it first. The prophet Isaiah states it this way, "Declaring the end from the beginning, and from ancient times *things* that are not *yet* done..." (Isaiah 46:10a). He puts inside of you everything necessary to get the most favorable outcomes that He has planned for every phase of your life. God plans "outcomes" when He is compiling "in-comes" (what He places inside of you).

Although we live in the present, God is not limited to the present. He lives outside of the clock and calendar. He is always in the present with you, but He is also already in next week. When you "get there" He will already "be there." God is never rushing you out of the present moment, but the reality is that this moment is fleeting. So, in order to live a great life we have to become good at "living in the present" while "thinking into the future." Because God is in the present and future at the same time, living in sync with Him should be a leading aim of our life. To stay connected to the one who knows what's next is a great life objective.

When God thinks of "what's next" for you, it always has a growth element attached to it. God is all about growth, increase, and advancement. When God speaks of your "tomorrow" it always involves advancement beyond your "today." If God is going to remove "one thing from you" it is only for the purpose of improving "all things around you." When God thinks of the next phase; the next era; the next level; He always has something better in mind.

If you are in your twenties approaching your thirties, expect the decade of your thirties to be better than your twenties. Likewise, your forties should be better than your thirties. If you are experiencing your amazing forties and thinking, "Nothing could top this," just wait until you enter the decade of your fifties. With each phase your wisdom kicks in at a higher level. You should have a better understanding of who you are and what you are all about. It should be easier to know what to say "yes" to and what to say "no" to. The older you get the better feel you will have for what kind of people you should connect with and what type of people to avoid. Your sense of judgment should be better and your ability to make wise decisions should be sharper.

God built into our life cycle the progression of moving from one place in life into something better. He is the author of graduating you to a higher level. When He thinks about your future it is a picture that is better than your present. The intent of God is clearly conveyed when He said, "Beloved, I wish above **all** things that thou mayest prosper..." (III John

1:2 KJV). God has a lot of aspirations for you, but He said He has one desire that He puts above all, and that is for you to prosper—to flourish—to advance. God desires this above everything! He longs for you to flourish; to advance; to do better. Transition is one of God's ways of bringing you into a better state.

2. If you stay at today, you will never experience the potential of tomorrow.

For the sake of this discussion, when I speak of today I am speaking of more than the calendar day. I am referring more broadly to a season—the present season of your life. You are living your life on the level to which you have come—the level of wisdom, experience, understanding, and maturity that you have attained. Your life is carried out in phases, or seasons. In an amazing life, great seasons are to be replaced by other delightful seasons. Life is a fascinating journey. In a journey, you never get to a place and remain there forever. You relish the best moments and continue the odyssey.

Years ago I came upon a season that I thought was going to be permanent. So, I unpacked the bags of my life and settled in. I thought, "Wow, I have finally arrived at the place where I no longer have to operate with high levels of focus, push to make something worthwhile happen, and hunt for uncommon opportunities." My prior focus of pushing and hunting finally brought me to that comfortable place. Then, unexpectedly, that season ended. Actually, it was replaced by a tougher season—one that required me to get back on the grind, put my hands back on the wheel, and push the pedal to the floor. I did not have the foresight to understand that the "first season" came to give me a jump on the "next season." The best time to prepare for war is during peace. I camped at the season of peace instead of using it to prepare me for the season of war.

The first lesson I learned from that experience was that seasons change. Often. I learned that I am to enjoy the current era with the understanding that it may not be permanent. Then, I was enlightened by the fact that even though a particular experience might be fantastic, destiny always has the potential for something even more sensational. God expresses this principal by speaking about His viewpoint of updating your revelation (the unveiling of truth), from one level to another. God takes you from the good, to the acceptable, to the perfect (See Romans 12:2). You will never experience the "acceptable" until you leave "good," and you will never experience the "perfect" until you advance from the "acceptable."

The greatest possibilities exist in front of you. You step into your potential. It is always in front of you—in your future. To walk into your potential is to walk beyond where you are currently at in your thinking and behaviors. All the possibilities are packaged in what you have not attempted yet. Perhaps the information you need to open you to broader possibilities is hidden in a class that you have been considering taking, or a research quest that you have yet to start. It could be that you are only a dozen phone calls from connecting with the person who not only has the know-how, but also the graciousness to make you their protégé. What if taking the step of membership in that organization is the missing puzzle piece to jolt you to a whole new level? In other words, you have to be willing to exchange your "present" for your "future." Exchange things like your comfort, your complacency, and your current way of thinking, to attain the best that is available, yet unrealized.

Hopefully, the current place to which you have come in life is a wonderful place. However, if you remain there you will never know what your potential has to offer you. Hold on to the positive qualities that are a reflection of the level that you are operating on and determine what parts of your make up you need to abandon in favor of greater possibilities. Does your list of things to abandon include failing to move forward as a result of feeling inadequate? Maybe you do not have the education that is typical for people who do what you are considering doing. Perhaps you feel that others know so much more than what you know. Or maybe you wonder if you will be taken as seriously because you do not have the credentials that normally accompany what you are thinking of attempting. Do you fear totally embarrassing yourself? Are you just intimidated by the vastness of the possibilities that are within your reach?

Let's consider this. What if all these are simply excuses because you are afraid of being as great as God is saying you could be? If there are things you do not know, you can learn them. A formal education is not a prerequisite for greatness. Be excellent—be great, and your education is not likely to come into question. Stop worrying about the spectators on the sidelines. They are not even in the game. They are watching you advance on the playing field of your destiny.

Let's stop making excuses for being great. Let's just take the steps of greatness. Every step should be a deliberate act of quality thoughts, intentions, decisions, and behaviors. Let's no longer be afraid to move into the unfamiliar, knowing that it is the unfamiliar that will transform our lives.

3. Transition causes a birthing of a whole new set of provisions.

Transition will take you into domains that you may not have operated in before. It will force you to think, process information, and respond in different ways than you did in your previous experiences. The purpose of transition is to elevate you. To raise the level of your thinking, worldview, experience, and life results. To walk in new worlds—new realms, you need new tools. That is, if you are going to be successful at navigating through transition, and advancing in life as a result of it.

Provision relates to a supply of something; especially of food. Biblically, food speaks of what you intake to sustain and advance you spiritually. Jesus said, "It is written, Man shall not live by bread alone, but by every word that proceeds from the mouth of God" (Matthew 4:4). There is a life outside of the obvious physical experience. It is your spiritual life—the life that provides meaning and perspective to your natural experience. If you do not have a spiritual food source you are starving the real you—the internal, spirit being that came from God. If you are deprived of food spiritually, your natural life will be destitute and be riddled with confusion, wandering, and uncertainty. Jesus made it clear where your spiritual nourishment is to come from—the mouth of God—the word of God. Not only the written word—the bible, but you must learn the art of asking God for guidance and hearing His specific answers and instructions.

When you find yourself in the midst of transition it will become evident that you need the food of the next level in order to successfully enter it. You will need next-level truth, information, wisdom (discernment of what to do), revelation (unveiled truth), and impartation (the transmission of power). My experience is this—if you are allowing God to orchestrate the journey of your life, the transitions that you find yourself in that you are cooperating with, automatically come with a set of new provisions. New truth and new wisdom present themselves. It then becomes your responsibility to latch hold of them and import them into your life operating systems.

I believe that what God initiates He sustains. If God is the one who put the order in, He is certainly going to pay the expenses associated with it. He will provide the new supplies and equipment necessary to navigate your way around the new world you are walking into.

If you are in transition and it seems that no new information, wisdom, revelation and impartation are showing up. Look harder, because new provisions accompany transitions that God orchestrates. When you become a serious seeker of what it is "you are going after," at some point it will start "going after you." Provision—everything you need to catapult you forward as you are navigating the transition you are in, will begin pursuing you. New information, revelation, wisdom and impartation will start showing up in your life. God never has a "vision" of where He is taking you without the "pro." If you put the two together you get pro-vision—"for the vision."

4. The first step away from your present is a step into your potential.

After two years of contemplation and prayer, I made the boldest move of my life. I announced that I was taking a different direction. Although I had primarily the same goal as the group of people that I had been associated with for the past twenty years, I would be taking a different path than them. It was a risky move because I was walking away from my support system.

I was not aware that God was orchestrating the most dynamic transition that I have ever experienced. Stepping away presented itself as a move that would weaken my journey. It tried to intimidate me. Stepping away from the group postured itself as a terrorist that threatened my demise if I made the decision to leave my present existence. It tried to compel me to stay and deter me from leaving. In addition to using fear and intimidation it made a great case for staying. But I knew I was supposed to go.

When I made the decision to step away from my "present" into my "future" the transition started. I said, "Goodbye," and turned and begin to walk away—into my future—into my potential. The first step I took shocked me. I felt something very powerful with that first step. I felt my world expand. I took another step. It happened again. I could literally feel my world expand even more. So much so, that after a handful of steps I looked to my left to see if there was something there. I was greeted with such a powerful sense of expansion that it instantly silenced two years of intimidation. I was instantly validated that stepping away from my present was not a step "into weakness," but a step "into strength."

After Moses died God gave Moses' servant Joshua some specific instructions. He said, "Moses My servant is dead. Now therefore, **arise, go** over this Jordan, you and all this people, to the land which I am giving to them—the children of Israel" (Joshua 1:2). The two key words in the instructions were arise and go. That's transition—get up and go. You have to take the first step away from what currently is. Every step away from today is a step towards what you could become.

After God gave Joshua the instruction He gave him a promise. He said, "Every place that the sole of your foot will tread upon I have given you, as I said to Moses" (Joshua 1:3). He did not say, "Every place that you can see I will give to you," He said, "Every place that your foot will touch." In other words, you have to leave where "you are at" and step into the place "you need to be." Your feet will only tread upon that which you have the faith to walk into. That is the ground that God will give you—the ground you were bold enough to walk into.

5. In Transition, you are not being punished, you are being promoted.

When you are in familiar surroundings you know what to

expect. Your "past experience" helps to predict your "present reality." If you are in a season where most of your experiences are fitting into the normal pattern and flow of your life, you have a feel for what a normal day is going to be like. You can let your guard down very easily and just enjoy the flow of the current chapter of your life. On the other hand, if you are in a season of transition, it takes the car of your life down roads you have never been before. It presents twists and turns that are unpredictable and unexpected at times. All of a sudden you are in unfamiliar territory.

At times it is like walking in a pitch black basement and desperately trying to locate that string hanging from the pull-chain light fixture. You make sure your footing is secure before you take another step and then you start reaching upward in the area where you believe the string is hanging. There are times where you move your hand all around, in an attempt to find the string, but have no success at locating it. You know it is in the area that you are reaching for, but it somehow eludes you. Then there are times when you bump the string, which causes it to start swinging, creating a game of cat-and-mouse with the pull string. You think you have a grip, only to discover the moving string has dodged you. You are in the dark desperately searching for some light—for some familiarity.

When you are in transition you are between "where you were" and "where you are going to be." You are in motion—headed somewhere. But the journey is not predictable. So it is common to have sensations of instability, aloneness, darkness, and uncertainty when you are in transition. These things can easily make you feel like you are being "demoted" instead of being "promoted." Be that as it may, transition never comes as a form of punishment, but rather a type of promotion. Although at times it does not "feel good," it "is good." God can, and will, use any situation you find yourself in to advance your life. If you are in a difficult, scary, or intimidating transition, just hold on, embrace the process, and expect promotion in some area of your life. I like the Psalmist David's eloquence when he said, "We went through fire and through water: but thou broughtest us out into a wealthy place" (Psalms 66:12b KJV). Let's learn to not focus more on the difficult "process" than we do on the glowing "profit" contained within it.

ADDITIONAL POWER POINTS

- Transition wraps "pleasant" surprises in "unpleasant" packaging.
- Sometimes the first step away from your present is the most powerful one. It shows you that you have the ability to walk in new and exciting terrains.
- Being between levels can feel lonely, boring, unending, and purposeless. Being between levels is traveling time on the way to the next best thing that God has for you.
- Don't be afraid to step into your future. God is already there…waiting for you.
- Whenever God thinks of the "next thing" for you it always has an element of the "best thing" for you.
- God is not the "punisher" He's the "promoter."

CHAPTER NINE
TRANSITION PRODUCES TRANSFORMATION

"The important thing is this—to be ready at any moment to sacrifice what you are for what you could become.[1]" Charles Dickens

A production center is a conglomeration of tools, systems and support mechanisms that are put in place to facilitate the production of a product or work of art. Transition is like a production center. Many wonderful "products" have come from its warehouse. One of the most fascinating things about transition is what is birthed as a result of it. Quite often the fruit of transition is the birthing of ideas, mindsets, concepts, and approaches that would have otherwise never been born.

There are certain experiences in life that force you to look at things from an entirely different angle than you ever even considered before. Sometimes the speed at which "life" comes at you does not allow you time to consider all the potential consequences of a decision, act or deed. When a certain decision produces unintended or unconsidered consequences, you are forced to think from a much broader angle than you did when you were making that decision with little or no time to consider all the ramifications.

The process of transition often reveals things about you that you otherwise would have never discovered. Becoming enlightened about some aspect of yourself that was hidden from you is one of the most powerful things you will ever experience. Years ago I was judgmental of a guy for his lack of respect for his wife. I thought, "This guy is so self-centered that he doesn't have the capacity to even consider his wife's feelings." A few years later I found myself in a major transition that forced me to spend a lot of time alone—looking inside. It was during that time that I discovered that I had demonstrated the same level of disrespect for my own wife. I could not see it at the time because I had placed myself in a position of mentally policing others while I was excluding myself from the scrutiny. The transition I was experiencing forced me into seclusion which positioned me to turn my glasses of surveillance towards me.

"Transition" should ultimately result in "transformation." If you cooperate with "the process" you are likely to experience an overhaul of the way you see yourself, God, and the world. In essence, transition should cause a transformation of your "self-view," "God-view," and "world-view."

Self-View
Although it is obvious that you know more about yourself than anyone else does, your viewpoint of how you really are may not be accurate. For instance, I recently had a series of interactions with an individual who strikes me as being blatantly arrogant and self-absorbed. However, he describes himself as being humble. There is a huge gap between the way he "views" himself and the way he "presents" himself. He presents himself in a "cocky" way, but views himself in a "humble" way. It is a dreadful thing to be the only one who is unaware of an obvious flaw that you have. To have a tainted self-view is to live in self-deception. Self-deception is like living with a handicap that you are totally oblivious to.

Transition has a way of presenting you with the facts—the facts about yourself. It has a way of awakening your vision. When I say, "vision," I'm not referring to what you see externally, I'm referring to your ability to see from within. I'm speaking of insight. I'm referencing perception. I'm talking about the quality of being able to view things accurately—to see things the way they really are.

When one season of your life abruptly ends and you're forced to enter a new season, the "new season" requires "new vision." The way you saw things in the "past" is not likely to work well in the "present." When you find yourself in unpredictable times, where you are not sure where you're going or what's next, you need to start looking at things differently than you did before. It is a time for opening your eyes and assessing what brought you here and what your response to it should be.

Even more importantly than assessing circumstances is assessing yourself. When you find yourself in a season of turmoil or uncertainty, or a phase where something has ended that you can't go back to, you have no time for ignoring things about yourself that contributed to the chaos. Nor can you ignore things about you that have the potential of sabotaging your journey to your next chapter. Transition should trigger "self-assessment" that leads to "self-honesty." You must use this time to discover the dysfunctional things about yourself that you did not have the courage to confront in the past. The transition you are facing has probably already turned some area of your life upside down. While trying to determine what in the world is going on, you might as well look at yourself to determine if there's something about you that produced or attracted the drama.

The truth you discover about yourself may not be pretty. It may be revealed to you that you are deceptive, manipulative, jealous, dishonest, self-serving, self-centered, disloyal, and/ or petty. At some point you must confront yourself and be brutally honest with yourself. It is likely that you have some personal "issues" in some area of your life. The parts of you that you fail to deal with that are "messed up" are the very parts that will likely "mess you up." The flaw that you will not confront is the one most likely to produce the failure. If you are dealing with a weakness that you feel is "much bigger than you," and you are afraid that you do not have the ability to overcome it by yourself, make sure you reach out to someone for help.

The most important person to study is "you." The clearer you are about who you are and what you're all about, the less complicated your life becomes. When you start to fully understand yourself, you become empowered to know what to say "no" to and what to say "yes" to. You know who to connect with and who to avoid. It becomes clear where you should show up and what places and events you should avoid. Your life becomes streamlined. You also develop the keenness to remain conscious of your tendencies that have the potential of causing a mess of things.

Seeing yourself honestly and accurately is empowering. When you are no longer "self-deceived" you are less likely to be "man-deceived"—deceived by someone other than you.

God-View

In 1998 when I experienced the greatest transition of my life, I discovered a God who I had not known in the twenty-one prior years of my relationship with him. Maybe I should say I discovered an aspect of God that I had missed. The God I knew prior to the transition spoke to me primarily through someone else. When I entered a period of isolation, the God I discovered spoke to me without the aid of those who said they represented God's voice to me. "Transition" is often accompanied by "isolation." Isolation has a way of correcting "hearing loss" and "vision distortion." What God tries to communicate to you when you are in "crowded situations" can be drowned out by the sounds of confusion surrounding you. So God uses transition as a season of your life where you discover the God that you had heard about but never experienced. He is the God who speaks loudly when you are silent.

In 1992 a Christian song writer named Lynn Deshazo wrote a song called Be Magnified. The song starts with, "I have made You too small in my eyes O Lord—forgive me...²" God is "big," but if the view you have of Him is "small," your "experience" is going to be limited by your "perspective." The verse of that song implies that something occurred in the song writer's life that revealed to her that God was bigger than she had previously thought. Your transition will warrant you expanding your view of God and His capacity and competence to orchestrate the affairs of your life. One of the meanings of the name Jehovah is "the God who proves Himself." God does not "have" to prove Himself, He "chooses" to prove Himself. You must view Him as the God who proves Himself, and worship Him as the God who proves Himself. If you worship Him as your healer, Jehovah-rapha (the Lord who heals) will show up. If you worship Him as peace giver, Jehovah-shalom (the Lord is peace) will show up. The God that you worship is the one who will appear.

The song continues with "And I have believed in a lie—that You were unable to help me." Sometimes your situation seems so "messed up" that you do not believe it can be "cleaned up." It seems unfixable—even by God. It can even seem like God is not the answer. God is always the answer—just not the obvious one. Just because He's not making "noise" does not mean He's not making "moves." God's involvement is not always obvious. So the feeling that God is unable to help you is a "lie" that feels like the "truth." But you must remember that transition is about getting you from where you are to where you're supposed to be. So sometimes the areas of your life that have gotten "broken" were because they were never "fixed" in the first place. So God uses the transition you are facing to fix what was broken before you recognized that it was broken.

Recall in chapter two where I talked about "Dismantling." I stated, "You have to let go of what will no longer be useful and get rid of what will no longer be necessary." Dismantling is to allow room for remantling." So the truth is not only is God always the one who is able to help you, but He is probably orchestrating your movement from your "today" into your "tomorrow." You just have to change your view of Him as the "orchestrator" and not the "obstructer." His aim is to move you from stagnation to momentum.

God is so multifaceted that it is not likely we will ever discover every aspect of Him. Be that as it may, the potential tragedy is to view a God whom is "without limits" through eyes that are "accustomed to limits." In order to walk through transition you are going to have to walk past limits. Any viewpoint you have of God that has any hint of limit associated with it must be identified, confronted, and eliminated. All your assumptions about God's size, speed, and creativity must be open to scrutiny.

Your transition will take you into unchartered territory. Reach for Him in your most unsure and darkest places. God once said to one of his leaders, "And you will seek Me and find Me, when you search for Me with all your heart" (Jeremiah 29:13). You will discover the God who changes your view of Him when your transition provokes you to seek Him with all of your "heart" and not your "head." Keep reaching for Him until He shows up in your most unlikely place. He lives there too. You must discover the God who lives in "unchartered waters." Meet Him out there where you've never been before. You will never go somewhere that

God is not already at.

If your view of God is that He's a God who dwells in churches you will miss a lot of who He is. Although God "visits" buildings He does not "live" in them. You certainly do not have to wait until you enter a church building in order to encounter God. God will meet you right where you are—where ever that may be. He will meet you "where you are" and take you to "where you need to be." Transition represents movement. God is a God of movement. If you are in transition look for God—He's nearby. He is attracted to movement, development, and growth. The first thing He ever said to man was be fruitful (development), multiply (growth), and replenish the earth (movement).

World-View
As your view of yourself becomes illuminated and your view of God is enlarged, it will naturally expand the way you view life and everything associated with it. Have you ever done something for the first time and concluded that it was a fascinating experience? If so, has it ever caused you to conclude, "I could have made this a practice years ago and been enjoying an enhanced level of amusement, relaxation or thrill in my life?" You can have such a narrow view of life that you end up going to the same three or four places and doing the same two or three things for twenty or more years without giving thought to any alternatives. One of the byproducts of transition is that it tends to force you to revisit the way you look at how certain aspects of life works. When you revisit your past assumptions about how you think about and react to people, and view and respond to events and situations, you have the potential to discover new, more expanded perspectives.

There have been times when I had very strong views against a particular conduct or act until I discovered a family member or close friend to be found doing (or to have done) that very thing. Suddenly my viewpoint softened because the perpetrator was someone that I cared about. Because I had knowledge of their many positive qualities I quickly became more lenient in my judgment of them. In time I even became more sympathetic towards others who were known to be guilty of the same.

What's even more compelling is when one of your personal weaknesses or flaws produces a "slip up" that goes public and brings embarrassment and shame to you and those associated with you. Your wrongdoing and the pain that it causes should naturally produce a tenderness and empathy in you towards others who are dealing with the consequences of their mess ups. You may not have been as forbearing with others had you not experienced a desperate need for forbearance when you were in trouble.

The "new land" that your transition is taking you into will require "new eyes" through which you are viewing things. If you continue to look at things the way you have in the "past" you run the risk of not entering your "future." Transition is a time for reevaluating how you view women, how you view men, how you view people whose views differ from yours, how you view other races and cultures, and how you view your place in the global scheme of things.

Quite frankly, the world is made up of people. So actually, "your world" view is really your "people view"—it's the way you see people—and the way you relate to them. Within every human being lies some greater purpose that only God can fully know. There is something "good" even in the "worst" among us, even if you have to search hard and long to find it. Do not make the mistake of missing God in the person you encountered today.

What if you started treating each person that you encounter the way you would treat God if He was the person in front of you? If He appeared with tattered clothes or with a mental or physical impairment would you treat God with any less respect? What if God appeared and requested help right in the middle of something that was important to you? Would you lose patience or feel interrupted? What if you came to realize that God placed different levels of gifts in each person, and the full gift of those with mental or physical challenges is only fully expressed when you reach out to share your love and patience with them? What if your true value on earth was not measured by what you accomplished, but by how often you totally forsook your comfort in favor of tending to someone else's comfort?

Do not make the mistake of going through "transition" without allowing it to produce "transformation." Always look for the purpose for the madness. Whenever you find yourself in transition begin to relook at the way you view yourself, the way you see God, and the way you view the world.

ADDITIONAL POWER POINTS
- The real you is hidden somewhere on the inside of you waiting to be discovered by you.
- There are so many layers of you that it may take more than a lifetime to discover them all.
- God is too multifaceted to be fully understood, but His value warrants a valiant effort to discover all that you possibly can about Him.
- Your willingness to submit your pre-established assumptions about God to scrutiny positions you to discover facets of Him that were not previously on your radar.
- The way you view "others" is tied to how you view "yourself."

- The world is "smaller" than it used to be. Instead of your community being limited to your neighborhood, the entire world is now your community through social media.

CHAPTER TEN
NAVIGATING THROUGH TRANSITION

"We must eulogize what isn't supporting our purpose.[1]" L.T. Lewis

There are basically two ways that you can go through transition. You can take it as it comes, or you can navigate your way through it strategically. Being strategic always increases your likelihood of success. Although you cannot always predict all the nuances that your transition will throw at you, you can take on the proper mindset and establish a decisive approach to it. Navigating your way around implies that you are deliberate and purposeful as you take your journey. Here are some principles to keep in mind, as well as some do's and don'ts for successfully navigating through transition.

GOD WILL SOMETIMES CLEAN YOUR PLATE SO HE'S THE ONLY THING LEFT ON IT

Transition can be such a perplexing thing to understand. It can seem like it is "an enemy" when in fact it is an "a friend." For that reason, you must embrace the process, cooperate with it, and approach it thoughtfully. Transition will present some wonderful opportunities to you. Some of them are not as obvious as others. For example, some transitions are triggered by an event that results in you having to start over. Maybe an organization that you were a part of dissolved, or a relationship ended, or a move to a new town became necessary. Sometimes things in your life leave. Assignments, events and responsibilities dissolve. God will sometimes clean your plate so He's the only thing left on it. If that is the case, it is likely that God is calling you into a season of just being with Him. Enjoy it. Embrace it. God probably has some wonderful things that He wants to tell you and show you. It has the potential of being the most enjoyable season of your life.

A clean plate is a wonderful opportunity to rethink your options. It allows you to carefully pick and choose the things you are going to commit to as you proceed forward. A clean plate gives you the luxury to assess responsibilities that you took on in the past that turned out to not be "God assignments." That way you will not repeat the missteps that cluttered your plate. Having too much on your plate and having the wrong assignments on your plate can both produce a sense of chaos. Having a clean plate allows you be more discriminating in what you will say "yes" to. A clean plate produces a clear head. When God gives you a clean plate be careful what you put on it.

Someone once said, "People come in your life for a reason, a season, or a lifetime." You have to know who you are connected to and for how long. Sometimes people in your life leave. Some relationships are very temporary. Others are life-long. Some will last for a period of time, but with an expiration date on them. You have to determine who you are connected to and for how long. If someone is leaving your life, or if a relationship is ending *for whatever reason*, it could be that God is cleaning your plate, or streamlining your life. If the drama leaves along with the person, the "loss" turns out to be a "gain." Do not put a "comma" where God is putting a "period." Become more deliberate about assessing the ebb-and-flow of the relationships in your life.

There are times when a relationship is not totally severed; however, it is reduced—it is simplified. Fewer conversations and face-to-face visits are necessary to maintain the relationship. Allow your life to take on a flow and do not try to make something happen that is not occurring naturally.

STOP TALKING ABOUT THE THINGS THAT YOU WANT TO DIE—YOUR WORDS ARE KEEPING THEM ALIVE

Another important element of successfully navigating through transition is the focus of your conversations. Whatever dominates your mind normally dominates your conversations because words are an interpretation of your thoughts. Your words allow you to process your thoughts. The best way to keep a situation prominent and in the forefront is to keep talking about it. The best way to put something to rest is to discontinue talking about it. The popular proverb says, "Death and life *are* in the power of the tongue, and those who love it will eat its fruit" (Proverbs 18:21). Your tongue—your words, have the ability to keep something alive or put it to death. If your dilemma is the result of something that was done to you, something withheld from you, or something taken from you, it is tempting to make it known to whoever will listen. It might not be a bad idea to talk this through with your spouse, mentor, or someone who is mature enough to hear it and not become tainted. However, it may not be so wise to talk about it with every "Joe Blow" who will listen. The more you talk about a thing the more power you give it. If conversing about the matter only adds to your frustration, at some point you must stop talking about it. The proverb that says, "Death and life are in the power of the tongue," does not just say that "death" is in the power of your tongue, it also says "life" is. Your words can keep alive that which you want to die.

LET GO OF WHAT'S LEAVING

Every so often the end of a thing is inescapable. Fighting the inevitable is exhausting. Could you possibly be resisting the very thing that your destiny is trying to bring "to an end" because it wants to bring something better "to its beginning?" Sometimes we face the reality that the "new" and the "old" simply cannot coexist. So you have the "new" waiting for the exit of the "old." When that is the case, the "new" will not present itself until it sees the "old" leave the room.

There are times when what you are trying to keep has already lost its useful life, so you are in essence trying to carry something dead into your future. You have to discern if you should resist what's exiting or allow it. Sometimes it is more powerful to "cooperate" than it is to "compete." Let go of what's leaving. Anything that leaves was not yours permanently anyway. Anything that leaves your life does you a favor by allowing room for something greater to come along and replace it.

Now the loss of a loved-one does not apply to this principle. Losing someone close to you is a loss that you are not trying to easily get over. There is a grieving process that is normal and advisable. I do not believe that you should totally let them go. Although they have passed away you can still keep them alive. They can always be as close to you as the wonderful thoughts and memories that you have of them.

If the transition you are facing is that of navigating through the loss of a loved-one I would like to suggest that you do three things—grieve their loss, assess what you gained, and determine what piece of their life you are to pick up and carry forward.

Chapter 10

Grieve Their Loss

Grief is the natural reaction to loss. Grief is processing your feelings and emotions. It is a strong, sometimes overwhelming emotion. You might find yourself feeling numb and removed from daily life, while burdened down with your sense of loss. Although you may feel sick, grief is not an illness. Grief helps you to let go of the past and adjust to a new life without the person who died. All people grieve differently. Some people will feel shocked and numb in the beginning. Strange and painful thoughts and feelings may follow—thoughts of confusion, disbelief, and wondering if this is just a dream may ensue. You may experience feelings of sadness, anger, guilt, loneliness, bitterness, fear, edginess, nervousness, short tempered, and lack of confidence. All of these feelings are natural.

King David in the bible was grieving his son's eminent death. He was lying on the ground and would not get up, eat, or talk. At some point he got up and proceeded forward. The account reads, "So David arose from the ground, washed and anointed himself, and changed his clothes; and he went into the house of the LORD and worshiped. Then he went to his own house; and when he requested, they set food before him, and he ate" (II Samuel 12:20). At some point you will need to do like David—get up, put some clothes on, wash your face, go to God's house and give Him praise, because there is something therapeutic about worship.

So first, you grieve the loss, and then you assess what you gained.

Assess What You Gained

When someone close to you dies you hear repeatedly, "Sorry for your loss," "Sorry for your loss." It certainly was a loss. However, their life was a gift to you, which would mean there was so much that you gained. You have to assess what you gained. What did you gain? What did she say to you that no one else said? What did his handshake feel like? What did she transmit to you when she touched you? Every life has a message. Every life is a message. What message did her life give you? What did he impart to you? How is your life better because of what she left with you? First, you grieve the loss, and then you should assess what you gained. The next thing to do is to determine what piece of their life you are supposed to pick up and carry forward.

Determine What You Will Carry Forward

What part of their life will you keep alive? Is it an attitude that uplifted you, a mindset that always appealed to you, or an approach that inspired you? What is it about them that you know you are to keep alive in some way?

You are not trying to be them. You are allowing their life to help transform your life. You are allowing their inspiration to give birth to improvement and enhancement in your life. Maybe something about their life is what will birth a new powerful perspective, a new focus, or a new approach that upgrades your life and enhances the life of those around you.

Grieving the loss of a loved-one, assessing all that you gained from them, and then determining what aspect of their life will fuel some area of your life provides you with a thorough process for navigating that very difficult terrain.

ELIMINATE SCATTERED THINGS THAT ARE MAKING YOUR JOURNEY THROUGH THE WILDERNESS LABORIOUS

When things get "disordered" they cause "disorientation." When things have been removed from their proper place and left scattered around, it becomes difficult to locate them when needed again. In other words, it's hard to operate when you cannot find things in their proper place. What's even more chaotic is when things that have gotten out of place begin to pile up in a discombobulated mess. It becomes difficult to think clearly when surrounded by clutter. If you cannot "think clearly" it is difficult to "act decisively."

When you are in midst of leaving something that has ended that you can't return to, while moving toward something else that has started but you have not yet arrived at, the last thing you need is to make the journey with things that impede your progress. Transition is travel. On this journey you do not want to "pack heavy," you want to "travel light." You must make sure you get rid of any clutter in your life that may interfere with or obstruct the path that you are traveling on. You must also make sure that your heart and mind remain free from things that obstruct their ability to receive the messages that God is transmitting. Get rid of any and all clutter.

Let me expand your perspective of what clutter is. Old routines that have reached their expiration date are clutter. Places that no longer inspire are clutter. People that bring you down are clutter. Negative environments are clutter. Scattered things are also known as clutter. People who drain you dry are clutter. Assignments that God did not give are clutter. Unforgiveness is clutter. Even a clouded mind is clutter. Clutter takes up your best space and disallows room for God's best for you. Wherever there is "clutter" there is "confusion." Wherever there is "confusion" there is "stagnation." You cannot afford to be stagnant in this season. So it's time to eliminate scattered things that are making your journey through the wilderness laborious.

DON'T BE LATE DURING TRANSITION

Transition is not a time to be inattentive, sloppy or

nonchalant. When you are maneuvering through crucial periods of your life you must do so alert and attentive. You must display a healthy respect for the transition that you find yourself in. One way to show respect for the transition that you are facing is to be time conscious. Show up early to all events and appointments during transition. I learned from Dr. Undrai Fizer that if you are habitually late, your life will be late. The things that you need will not show up on time. They may show up way past the deadline when it's too late for them to be really beneficial. You are teaching your life to mirror what its master is doing. When you are in transition you cannot afford to have the things you need "today" to arrive "tomorrow." Don't be late during transition.

DON'T WASTE ENERGY DEBATING DURING TRANSITION

When you are in a season of transition it is not a season for fighting and debating with others. That is not a good use of your energy. As a matter of fact, a high demand is probably being placed on your energy resulting from the financial, mental, psychological, interpersonal, spiritual, physical, or relational changes associated with your transition. This is not the time to be wasting energy—especially on useless arguing and disputing. Your "best energy" must be used for creating your "best momentum."

What sense does it make to squander time trying to explain your transition to others when you may not fully understand it yourself? To try to explain to a detractor why you left an organization, severed an unhealthy relationship, or moved to a new city can sap you of the little energy you have left. The time for "creating your future" is not the time for "debating your past." When you are in transition don't debate—create. Transition is a time for re-creating, re-arranging, re-newing, re-storing, re-structuring, and re-vising.

OUTTHINK YOUR CIRCUMSTANCES

One of the most powerful things that you can do is to think. I mean getting away from everything just to think. Just like to you go to the spa to get pampered, or to the gym to work out, you should go to a quiet place to think. Make sure you have a pad of paper and something to write with. When you are alone you can find thoughts arising from a place within you that when you are in public is dormant and inaccessible. When you get alone you can experience an interior environment that is private and uninfluenced by the noise from the external world.

Sometimes it seems as if your circumstances have put together a strategy for you without your input? It's almost as if your circumstances have sat around and put thought into what they are going to throw at you. It would be a tragedy to let your circumstances have more of a say in your life than you do. That is why when you are in transition it is so vital to be deliberate about getting away to think. You do not want to approach the next moment blindly. Put some thought into what just happened, and why it occurred. If the situation you are facing is adverse, think about what you need to put in place to prevent it from happening again in the future. Determine if there are some potential "aftershocks" that might arise behind this "earthquake" you just went through. Think about how you might prepare for those aftershocks so you will not be caught off guard. Begin thinking about intelligence that would have prevented the situation you find yourself in if you would have had access to it back then. Begin gathering and studying that data for your future. Think about who you need to discontinue talking to during this season, while determining who you need to put on speed dial. Gather what it is your destiny is trying to communicate to you during this transition. Take time to think. Get alone to think. As you spend time in thought you will begin to see a picture of what you need to do next. Then, you will be in position to plan your next move before your future does it without your input. You will be poised to outthink your circumstances.

Navigating through transition is just that—it's a voyage. You are in unchartered territories. You must be alert and attuned. You must live awake. You have to keep your eyes wide open and your senses sharp. You have to become more deliberate and strategic. You have to know what the do's and don'ts are and strictly adhere to them.

ADDITIONAL POWER POINTS
- Don't allow people, places, and things into your space that damper your peace, pace, and productivity.
- If it doesn't inspire let it expire.
- The tough waters that you successfully navigate through in the "present" are ones that can't drown you in the "future."

CHAPTER ELEVEN
MUST HAVES WHEN IN TRANSITION

"It's the friends you can call up at 4 a.m. that matter.[1]"
Marlene Dietrich

A seasoned hiker would never take a trip into the wilderness without packing certain items. As a matter of fact there are things that are considered essential when taking such a journey. There is something known as the ten essentials. The original Ten Essentials list was assembled in the 1930s by The Mountaineers, a Seattle-based organization for climbers and outdoor adventurers, to help people be prepared for emergency situations in the outdoors. The Ten Essentials are[2]:

1. Navigation (a map & compass)
2. Sun Protection (sunglasses/sunscreen)
3. Insulation (extra clothing)
4. Illumination (headlamp/flashlight)
5. First Aid
6. Fire (waterproof matches/lighter/candles)
7. Repair Kit & Tools
8. Nutrition (extra food)
9. Hydration (extra water)
10. Emergency Shelter

On a routine trip you may use only a few of the items. However, if you are wandering in the wilderness, you have no idea which item(s) could actually end up helping you stay alive. Depending on the situation, failure to have one important item could turn out to be fatal to your survival in the wilderness. For that reason, first you must "know what to pack," and then you need to make sure that you "pack what you know." This list of necessary items suggests that the wilderness is not only an adventure, but can be outright dangerous. Especially if you have not packed the essentials.

Being in transition can feel like being in the wilderness. Not only can it "feel" like it—it can "be" like it. For that reason you need to be prepared for the unpredictable rocky terrain of transition. Let me offer some must haves when entering the wilderness of transition. When in transition the three must haves are the right focus, the right people, and the right environment.

The Right Focus
Your life will move in the direction of what you are focusing on the most—either good or bad. That is why it is so important to have a focus. You see, your focus determines what you are currently putting energy into and it also defines what you refuse to spend time on. You need to define what your focus is during this season. By default, when you define your "focus" you identify your "distractions." One of the best ways to eliminate distractions is simply being pointed about what you are focusing on at the present time.

It is important that you have—not just any focus, but the right focus—when you are in transition. In chapter two I said, "If you put all of your focus on the "mess" you will miss the "message." Some of the best things that "come from you" will be when something unpleasant is "happening to you." So, you want to avoid putting all of your attention on the wilderness that you find yourself in and focus on what your destiny is teaching you as a travel through it.

You can be forced into transition with little or no warning.

At times you just find yourself in transition—along with the realization that you have to stand up and face your new reality. The good thing is that transition has a built-in educational system that can instruct and enlighten you with the wisdom you need to break into your next era. In chapter two I said, "Crisis is a university—a literal educational institution designed for information and instruction. It uncovers where you were unguarded. It notifies you about weak structures that you thought could hold you up under the scrutiny of adversity, but turned out to be unreliable. It advises you about your lack of judgment. It teaches you the areas that you can never "go to sleep on" again. It informs you of the disciplines that you will be required to put in place in order to not repeat the current tragedy. It infuses you with an alertness that you never would have gained without the dilemma you faced. It schools you in the art of preparedness for future trouble. Crisis exposes your vulnerabilities so you can shore up your fragile areas in time for the next challenge. It trains you to put safeguards in place for the future that were not in place in the past."

Transition is a school. When you are in transition, consider the reality that you are in school. That should be your focus. You should be focusing on the education that transition is exposing you to and imparting in you. Your focus should be on what the professor *called transition* is lecturing on. Focus on the educational institution called transition and all of its advanced level courses.

Another great focus to have when in transition is on alignment—aligning your life with God's life. Focus on liking what God likes and hating what God hates. Focus on caring about what God cares about. The more your life is aligned with God, the more things will come in alignment with you. Things that seem chaotic will start coming into order. Things that are missing will start being found. Things that are broken will start being fixed. If you are in alignment with God then things associated with your life should recognize the alignment and follow suit. The closer you are to what God is like the closer you are to getting the results that God gets. Focus on what transition is teaching you and focus on getting your life in alignment with God.

The Right People
Being with the wrong people can sabotage your destiny. Being with the right people can catapult you into your destiny. You must become guarded and purposeful about the people you are associating with when you are in transition. You should become clear about who you need to "avoid" and who you want to "pursue." Let me suggest three types of people you must have when you are in transition. You need friends, fighters, and forerunners.

Friends
When you are in transition you will require a non-judgmental climate. For that reason you will need a friend, or a set of friends. Let me define friends. Friends love you for who you already are. Friends are not trying to make you something other than "what" you already are, or someone other than "who" you are. Friends are non-judgmental. Friends just love you. They do not try to change you—they leave that up to mentors. You will need a friend to be there to soothe you while your emotions are running all over the place. You will need someone who will "love you" when you are "not feeling the love." You will need someone who will comfort you when you are not feeling comfortable. Jesus understood this very well when He was preparing to leave his followers. He told them, "And I will pray the Father, and He shall give you another Comforter, that he may abide with you forever" (John 14:16 KJV). The Comforter is also known as the Holy Spirit—the Spirit of God (Luke 4:18). He is someone you want to add to your friend list when you are in transition.

He is totally non-judgmental. He is also known as the Spirit of Truth (John 14:17). You are going to need the truth, the whole truth, and nothing but the truth, when you are in transition. Your speculation about "the whys" of transition is not going to cut it. The Holy Spirit knows "the exactly" of it *if you will*. He is the voice of God (Revelation 2:29). You will need to hear God's voice as you are walking through this apparent unstable period. The Holy Spirit is also known as a defender (Isaiah 59:19). You will need a "supernatural" defender as you are experiencing turbulence in the "natural."

So you will require earthly friends and a heavenly friend. Your heavenly friend is already identified as the Holy Spirit—the Spirit of God. So, start to develop your relationship with Him. Talk to Him, ask Him questions and seek His guidance. Then, you will need to identify who your earthly friends are. They must meet the high standard of you knowing you can trust them unequivocally.

Fighters
When you are in the trenches you need to know you have someone who will get dirty with you. That is the definition of a "fighter." A fighter is an ally. They are someone who will fight with you. They will even fight for you if you do not have the strength to do it for yourself. A fighter is someone who "has your back." They are on your team and are ready to go to battle with you and for you without requiring a lot of detail. They are always "at the ready." All they need to know is that you need for them to fight with you and they immediately get engaged. They fight with prayer; they fight with defending your name and your position; they fight in any way that helps to protect you and advance you.

If you are looking to identify a spiritual warrior do not look for someone who just prays—look for someone who prays and gets results. Look for someone who has a connection to heaven. Solicit someone who has a strong connection to heaven and a heart for you.

Forerunners

A forerunner is someone who has walked through the transition you are currently in, and successfully come out on the other side of it. Begin searching for your forerunner. Your forerunner already knows what you have yet to discover. They can tell you what to expect, what to watch out for, and what to avoid. A forerunner can accelerate your progress. They can both excite and assure you. They can excite you about the promotion that is imminent, and assure you that you are going to make it through your seemingly insecure and unpredictable time.

When God sent an angel to the Virgin Mary to announce to her that she would become pregnant with the Son of God, Mary asked how would that be possible. After the angel explained it to her he told her to go see her cousin Elizabeth who was already six months pregnant even though everyone considered her old and barren. When you are in transition you need "an Elizabeth"—someone who is already pregnant with what it is you are trying to produce. You need someone who can sit you down and tell you, "At first you are not going to "feel" pregnant although you are going to "be" pregnant. Shortly after that you may start feeling nauseated—they call it "morning sickness." But relax honey, it won't mean that you're "sick"—it will be a sign that you're "pregnant." Then you will eventually start showing, and everyone else will be able to see that you are carrying a baby. Then you'll start "spreading." Your nose will spread and your hips will spread. When it's time to deliver that baby you will start having contractions, and those contractions will become so intense that you'll think you're gonna' die. But you're not gonna' die—it's just that what you become pregnant with will grow so big on the inside that there's no more room for it to stay in the womb anymore. And when that baby finally comes, the joy of your child will outweigh the memory of your pain."

That is how your Elizabeth talks to you. She takes you through the details of what to expect. She helps you to approach your future with confidence. She coaches you based on her actual experiences and expertise. She assures you that the process is a part of your destiny. She assures you that you will make it. You need an Elizabeth! You need a forerunner!

The Right Environment

Before God made man He created an environment to place him in. That is how important environments are. Your surroundings produce after their own kind. Where you reside is a great predictor of who you will become.

When you are in transition you will experience enough change for it to produce a bumpy ride. When that's the case, the last thing you need is an environment that contributes to the turbulence. You will need to be in quiet environments. By quiet I do not necessarily mean "free of noise"—I mean "free of conflict." Using energy to fight useless battles never promotes progress. It drains you. What "drains you" will never "sustain you." You must aggressively avoid atmosphere's that are riddled with conflict. Those places rob you of your best focus. They keep you on that proverbial treadmill—moving but going nowhere. Not only do quarreling environments stifle your progress—they regress your progress—they cause you to go backwards. Transition is all about moving forward, from your "present" into your "future." So, you cannot afford to be in environments that promote "regression," you must frequent places that promote "progression."

When you are "going places" you want to avoid environments where everyone is "going nowhere." People who are in prison with no hope of getting free love to keep others bound with them. They have no incentive for helping you get free when they have no plans to do so themselves. So avoid environments where the people love to see you staying the way you have always been.

You need environments that support progress—environments that support movement. This is a good time to reassess the health of the groups, committees and organizations that you are involved with. When determining your involvement with institutions, organizations or groups of people, you want to make sure your affiliation does not sabotage your effort to get from "where you're at" to "where you're supposed to be." The places you go to and the people you connect with should "reinforce" your progress, not "restrict" it.

If you cannot find the right environment, then create it yourself. Start gathering all the books, articles and teachings that you can find that speak to the transition you find yourself in. Create your own special place that you can go to and read, study, strategize and meditate.

ADDITIONAL POWER POINTS
- Never go into the wilderness without packing what may be necessary to get you out of it.
- The focus you are able to establish is a predictor of the progress you will be able to attain.
- In order to get the "right" relationships you may have to get rid of the "wrong" ones.
- What you learn in the "crisis" is what you will use to produce a "calm."
- The environments that "you hang out in" produce the environments that "hang out in you."

CHAPTER TWELVE
THE NEW YOU

"One day, when YOU wake up in the morning, YOU will find yourself taking a drive to your pleasure instead of maneuvering the vehicle in order to park "where you despise!'" Dr. Undrai Fizer

One of the most powerful seasons of my life was the season when I started to realize who I was and what I was all about. I went through a process of studying myself and developing the ability to articulate who I was. I finally came to the realization that I am all about communication, organization, preparation and revelation. I am wired to communicate information in a clear, concise and creative manner. I love the process of bringing order to the space around me and to the chaos of life. I thrive off of preparing for the assorted scenarios that life can throw at me. And, I live to uncover and discover empowering and enlightening truths.

Discovering who I am and being able to articulate it has taken a great deal of the mystery out of why I am here. I am here to "be" the person that I have discovered that God meticulously designed me to be. The more I simply "be" who He already made me, the more powerful I am. One of the greatest discoveries that I have made is that of finding "me."

Transition is "the great locator." It will "locate" you—it will pinpoint where your "head" is at and where your "heart" is at. It will uncover how you have been thinking, along with what is on the inside that is influencing your process of thought. It will expose where you are strong and where you are weak. Transition has a way of opening you up. Once you are open, have the courage to look inside. Once you look inside, have the bravery to be transparent with yourself about what you find.

It is important to enter a season of awareness—a season of becoming aware of yourself. You should take time to recognize what is "right" with you and what is "wrong" with you—where you are "skilled" and where you are "flawed." If your flaw presents itself in a way of thinking or behaving that results in negative outcomes, you have to confront your weakness and take aggressive steps to change it. It is easier to discover your flaws than you think. The people around you already know what they are. If you are not clear about what they are, ask the people closest to you. There are probably people in your life that are keenly aware of your flaws and would like to tell you about them, but they have never been given permission to do so.

When you identify your major flaw and bring judgment to it, and then take action to change it, your brilliance will have more room to materialize. It is important to give your brilliance as much space as possible so that what is "right" about you has a much bigger stage than what is "wrong" with you. You see, the season of transition is also the season of discovering your power—your strengths. Begin to clarify what your capabilities are, where your ingenuity shines, and where your expertise unfolds. Then you can structure your life around your strengths and find ways to multiply them.

As you are in a season of awareness and self-honesty, ask yourself if you have a tendency of blaming others for your circumstances. If so, stop blaming. By blaming others you are saying that they are the ones with the power. If you habitually blame others you relinquish your power over to those who you are citing as being responsible for your circumstances. Take responsibility for where you are at. "Own your stuff." Recognize that where you are at is a function of the sum total of whom you "are," or a result of who you have not yet "become."

The process of becoming aware of who you are can be a lengthy one. You must understand that there are so many layers to you that it will take more than a lifetime to discover all that you are. Give yourself time. Enjoy the process—take pleasure in the unearthing—both the good and the bad. If you fail to identify what is wrong, then there is little likelihood of removing it. Discovering your "dysfunction" is the beginning point of removing it. "Removing" it is the beginning point for "replacing" it.

One of the most powerful by-products of transition is the "you" who walks through transition and the "you" who entered it are usually entirely two different people. Your transition will demand things of you that your prior era never required. "Higher levels" always require more of you than "prior levels." The prerequisite for progress and advancement is that you become more than you currently are. The process of transition will force you to reach for answers, information and solutions that you otherwise would not have pursued had you not been thrust into transition.

In order to have a successful transition you will be required to become more aware than you were prior to your transition. You will need to be more aware of yourself, and more discerning of the new people you are encountering. Successful transition will place a demand on you to heighten your alertness—particularly if your lack of attentiveness resulted in your current chaos. Or, your current chaos may not have been the result of a lack of awareness. It may have been the result of dull instincts that failed to prompt you to "take action," or missed alerting you when you should have "stepped back from the action." Successful transition also necessitates higher levels of honesty and openness. You must first "come clean" with yourself and then come clean with those around you. Once you come clean with those with whom you interact, you must remain clean—stay open and honest. There is not a better time than now to quit playing games with people and with yourself.

Successful transition will also demand higher levels of wisdom than before. What you "know" brought you to where you are at—what you "need to know" is what is going to take you to where you need to be. So this season is not so much about "what you already know" as it is about "what you are able to discover." Discovery happens to those who are in the process of looking. The best way to discover truth is by becoming a serious seeker of it. I call it the law of productivity. Have you noticed that once a person who was having a hard time finding a job gets one, other employers suddenly become interested in them? It's easier to get a job when you already have one. When you are productive—when you are in motion, what you were seeking will eventually start seeking you. When you become a serious student of the wisdom you need to successfully navigate your way through your transition, your teacher will emerge.

When you increase your awareness, boost your alertness, embrace honesty and openness, and escalate your pursuit of wisdom, you will have become an entirely different person than the one who entered the transition. The "you" who solves a problem is an entirely different person than the "you" who encountered it. The awareness, alertness, honesty, openness and wisdom it took to overcome it, elevates you to a higher class individual than the person who was not required to have those qualities a short time before.

Transition is intelligent. It has a purpose. Although it seems like "it has a mind of its own," transition has a distinct objective behind it. Transition's aim is to always lead you into an improved state. Transition is always about advancing you. Transition supports your destiny. It comes along side of your destiny and says, "I will use what is happening "outside" of you to change something "inside" of you." "I am trying to upgrade your thinking." My aim is to reform your viewpoint." "I am all about enhancing the way you view things, and the way things view you."

Now it is important to understand that transition is not the "event." It is not what happens to you, but how you allow what happens "to you" to produce change "in you." Transition can work with "tragedy" or "triumph." It can work with anything that life throws at you to overhaul the way you approach life forever. If you are forced out of an organization that is integral to your life, you will land in transition. The leaving of the organization is not the transition—your reply to it is. Your mental response to the cutting of the ties becomes a part of the transition. Forging ahead with a sense of detachment is a part of the developmental process called transition. Learning to replace the voids that your disconnection produced is a reality of transition. Discovering that sometimes allowing a void to remain is better than putting something in its place can be a discovery of transition. Realizing that what you thought was a "void" that limited you, turned out to be "space" that protected you, can be an epiphany that transition produces. Transition is always trying to deliver something to you that you need to enhance your life.

START ACTING LIKE THE PERSON YOU WERE GOING TO GIVE YOURSELF FIVE YEARS TO BECOME

If you are like most people you have a vision of a better "you" than the "you" you are familiar with today. You have thoughts of self-improvement. You have dreams of a "future" that is better than your "present." Be that as it may, most of us take a long time getting to the improvements that we need to make. It is common to think that you always have time to initiate improvements. However, if you keep waiting until the "future," then your future will become your "present" and you will remain stagnant and void of growth. So what transition does is it breaks into your life and forces you to respond to life's ups-and-downs, and ins-and-outs. It demands that you dust off your creativity, savviness, organization and focus, so you can navigate your way through this maze that you find yourself in. It appeals to your more structured "you"; your more discerning "you." It insists on you staying alert and being deliberate. It requires you to find the people in your life that are "missing" and dismiss the people in your life who are "messing." Transition forces you into acting like the person you were going to give yourself five years to become. It accelerates your advancement to a better "you."

THE "YOU" WHO ASKS FOR SOMETHING GREAT AND THE "YOU" WHO RECEIVES IT ARE TWO DIFFERENT PEOPLE

If you are a renter and you ask God to help you become a home owner, you have to take on the characteristics of a homeowner in order to qualify to become one. If you are single and want to be married, you have to become a wife in order to attract a husband. When you become a wife, your husband will appear. If you are a bank teller and you want to move into selling investment products, you have to take on the qualities of an investment representative. Many people seek the title first. They want to wear the badge, carry the business card, and use the impressive title in their email signature line. You should not concentrate on the title. You should concentrate your energy on embodying the characteristics of the person who has the title. When you begin to look like, think like, structure like, organize like, and produce like the individuals who have that title, eventually people will begin to address you as a manager, or minister, or teacher, or attorney, or registered nurse. At some point people will start to address you by a particular title before it has officially been given to you. You became it; you functioned as it; you qualified for it, and then "it" attached its title to you. That is what transition will do "to" you and "in" you. It will naturally push you into developing your ability to navigate tough terrains, repair broken situations, insulate against repeated fiascos, and beckon uncommon insight. In the process you are being promoted to a higher level person.

As you are changing you will have to be watchful of people from your past. People from your past will try to relate to the "old you" because they have not been briefed on the "upgraded you." If they have not seen you in a while they are likely to refer back to their old reference of you—not realizing that God has substantially upgraded you. Even you have to understand that you are being upgraded by the minute; by the hour; by the day; by the week.

When you are in transition and you are cooperating with the metamorphosis process, you will start developing into a better "you." You will start to notice a more discerning you; a more alert you; a more deliberate you; a more attuned you; a more refined you. Transition forces you into a season of breaking habits, customs, and becoming free of other peoples opinion about you. You will eventually become so engrossed in the developmental process of transition that you may forget to even consider other people's opinion of you. As a matter of fact, you will begin to change at a rate where you may need to slow down and become familiar with the new person that you are becoming.

THE REAL ISSUE IS NOT THE PROBLEM YOU ARE FACING—THE REAL ISSUE IS THE NEW PERSON YOU ARE BECOMING AS A RESULT OF IT

Maybe your transition was triggered by the loss of a job. Maybe it was initiated by the loss of a loved-one. Perhaps an important relationship in your life fell apart. It could be that you are battling a major illness. It may be that you have been forced to leave a group of people who are as close to you as family members. Maybe you are facing divorce. Your career may have necessitated you moving to a whole new city by yourself. You may be entering retirement, or making the transition from a youth to a working adult. Maybe you are a first-time parent. Or your transition may be triggered by a number of unmentioned occurrences. Your focus; your energy; your best thoughts, your emotions—have all been aimed at the details associated with your transitional challenge. All along you have been thinking that the issue at hand was the specific challenge you have been dealing with. When in actuality, that is not the real issue. The real issue is not the problem you are facing. The real issue is the new person that you are becoming as a result of it. God simply used what you were going through to produce a whole new "you." If your transition was never triggered, your powerful response to it would have never come about. Your transition is forcing you to become something greater than you have ever been. You thought the victory was in successfully navigating through transition, when the real gift is the new "you." The greatest gift that you will ever receive from transition is the new "you" that it is producing. Get ready to discover the new "you." Learn how to articulate your new identity and enjoy its impact on the world.

ADDITIONAL POWER POINTS

- When you know "where you're at" *in life*, you better position yourself to know "where you're going."
- As you study so many things in the world around you don't forget to become an expert on who YOU are.
- One of the most powerful things that you can do is to change.
- The more aware you become of who you are and what you're about, the more aware you become of everything else.
- When you stop being blind to your flaws your life will start to reveal other lies that you are believing.
- There is a brilliant "you" on the inside waiting to be revealed—first to you, and then to the world.

REFERENCES:

The Introduction
1. *http://www.brainyquote.com/quotes/authors/r/r buckminster fuller.html, (accessed August 2, 2014)*

Chapter One
1. *http://www.brainyquote.com/quotes/quotes/h/ hughprathe107702.html?src=t change (accessed December 16, 2014)*
2. *http://www.landofbasketball.com/chapionships/, (accessed July 12, 2014)*

Chapter Two
1. *http://www.brainyquote.com/quotes/quotes/j/ joelosteen579095.html?src=t positive (accessed December 16, 2014)*

Chapter Three
1. *http://www.brainyquote.com/quotes/quotes/a/ alanwatts386511.html, (accessed September 2, 2014)*
2. *This paragraph on "change" was drawn from a message by Dr. Lance Wallnau, at the 2009 Ministers and Missions Conference, March 26, 2009, on "Convergence." Held at Living Word Christian Center, Forest Park Plaza, 7600 West Roosevelt Road, Forest Park, IL 60130. Conference Host: Bill Winston*

Chapter Four
1. *Undrai Fizer, Ph.D., The 365 (Divine House Books 2013), page 71*

Chapter Five
1. *http://www.brainyquote.com/quotes/quotes/n/ nicolausco238365.html, (accessed September 2, 2014)*
2. *J. Konrad Hole, Walking Through the Valley of Transition (World Press 1998), back cover.*
3. *Oswald Chambers, My Utmost For His Highest; The Classic Edition (Barbour Publishing, Inc. 1935), January 12 daily reading.*

Chapter Six
1. *http://www.brainyquote.com/quotes/quotes/k/ kristinarm569030.html, (accessed November 17, 2015)*
2. *http://www.uscrossier.org/pullias/wp-content/ uploads/2012/06/king.pdf, Letter from Birmingham Jail, by Dr. Martin Luther King, Jr, accessed August 16, 2014*

Chapter Seven
1. *http://www.goodreads.com/work/quotes/16278836-the- truth-about-butterflies-a-memoir, (accessed September 3, 2014)*
2. *The scientific facts about the caterpillar & butterfly were drawn from the article by Jo Price, "How does a caterpillar turn into a butterfly?" September 15, 2012, accessed 8/6/14. http://www.discoverwildlife.com/british-wildlife/how-does- caterpillar-turn-butterfly*

Chapter Eight
1. *http://www.brainyquote.com/quotes/quotes/t/ tomstoppar132715.html, (accessed November 17, 2015)*

Chapter Nine
1. http://www.wisdomquotes.com/quote/charles-dickens-4.html, (accessed November 17, 2015)
2. Lynn DeShazo, Copyright © 1992 Integrity's Hosanna! Music/Adm. by worshiptogether.com Songs excl. the UK, adm. by Integrity Music; CCLI Number: 645914

Chapter Ten
1. https://twitter.com/kbbevangelist, L.T. Lewis tweet dated 4/26/15

Chapter Eleven
1. http://www.goodreads.com/quotes/9479-it-s-the-friends-you-can-call-up-at-4-a-m (accessed November 19, 2015)
2. This information was drawn from the article by the REI Staff titled, "The Ten Essentials" on the Recreational Equipment, Inc (REI) website, last updated 2/10/15, accessed 9/14/15. http://www.rei.com/learn/expert-advice/ten-essentials.html

Chapter Twelve
1. Undrai Fizer, Ph. D., The 365 (Divine House Books 2013), page 17

CONNECT WITH
THE AUTHOR

I would love to interact with you and continue the dialogue about Transition, as well as other creative strategies and ideas to help advance your life to the next level.

Subscribe to my blog: *www.SpiritualLegislator.com*
Follow me on Twitter: *www.Twitter.com/@StanEllis2*
Like me on Facebook: *www.Facebook.com/stan.ellis.3910*
--Stan Ellis

CPSIA information can be obtained
at www.ICGtesting.com
Printed in the USA
FFOW05n1552120216